Michelle

AN AMERICAN STORY

Obama

Also by David Colbert

10 Days: Benjamin Franklin

10 Days: Anne Frank

10 Days: Thomas Edison

10 Days: Martin Luther King, Jr.

10 Days: Abraham Lincoln

10 Days: Albert Einstein

The Magical Worlds of Harry Potter

The Magical Worlds of The Lord of the Rings

The Magical Worlds of Narnia

The Magical Worlds of Philip Pullman

Eyewitness to America

Eyewitness to the American West

Eyewitness to Wall Street

Baseball: The National Pastime in Art and Literature

WWII: A Tribute in Art and Literature

Michelle

AN AMERICAN STORY

Obama

by
David Colbert

sandpiper
Houghton Mifflin Harcourt
Boston New York

www.sandpiperbooks.com

Hardcover ISBN 978-0-547-24941-4
Paperback ISBN 978-0-547-24770-0

Printed in the United States of America
DOC 10 9 8 7 6
4500739349

for Opla Lawrence

CONTENTS

INTRODUCTION

A year before the 2008 presidential election, a headline on the Washington, D.C., news website Wonkette asked, "Can Michelle Obama Be First Lady No Matter What?" At the time, Barack Obama was just one of many Democrats hoping to win the party's nomination. He was still introducing himself to the public. Hillary Clinton was expected to win the nomination easily. But Michelle already had her own fans. They had seen what other voters would soon learn: Michelle was every bit as refreshing as her husband. Possibly more so.

"There is no difference between the public Michelle and the private Michelle," says a friend. As Michelle's brother, Craig Robinson, put it, "Nothing is fake."

Here's what's real:

The first thing she told the White House housekeeping staff was, "My daughters are doing chores."

In her opinion, no one's mom and dad are better than her mom and dad. Maybe as good, but not better. Don't even think about it.

Her older brother still calls her for advice.

She's a hugger. A longtime friend says she connects with people one on one like nobody else. The most difficult kids melt when they talk with her. She's still friends with at least one of the children she met while running a day care center in college twenty-five years ago.

As sweet as she is with kids, she's that demanding of adults. When she was in elementary school, teachers who made promises they didn't keep heard about it from Michelle.

She has a temper. Fortunately for people who've

been on the receiving end, it disappears quickly.

That person you know from school who finished every assignment early? Michelle.

If there's a piano nearby and you ask right, she might play you the "Linus and Lucy" song from the "Peanuts" television cartoons.

She's more careful than Barack. Before he tried to convince voters that "Yes We Can," he had to convince Michelle.

Before the biggest speech of Barack's career, when he was unknown outside of his state and had been given the opportunity to open the 2004 Democratic National Convention, she calmed him down right before he went on stage by telling him, "Just don't screw it up, buddy."

She has made mistakes. A lot. Some of them more than once. She has an honors degree from Princeton and a law degree from Harvard, thanks to a lot of hard work, but at times she has wondered if she made the right choice to follow that path.

So where does it all come from? Michelle is full of confidence and will take on any task, but she truly believes she's ordinary. She thinks she is just a working mom who listened when her parents taught her to work hard. When she tells students they can be where she is, she means it. Sometimes Michelle gets annoyed when the press says she and Barack are special because they've accomplished so much. It can sound like the press is surprised Michelle and Barack could have gone to Princeton and Columbia and Harvard, or raised great kids. But that reaction is also part of Michelle's personality. She knows a lot of people who are doing the same thing, and she thinks they should be noticed. She's saying, *Hey, look at my friend over here.*

But of course Michelle and Barack aren't ordinary in every way. What they've achieved is unique. Yes, Michelle is just a working mom who shops online to save time. She's also the first White House resident to descend from slaves. That matters, and she knows it.

Michelle's family story goes back to the rice plantations of South Carolina, which were notoriously deadly. It follows the path of America through the Civil War and freedom, the Jim Crow segregation laws, the Great Migration of African Americans to cities in the north, the civil rights movement of the 1960s, and the women's movement. No other resident of the White House can say that, not even

Barack. Barack's family—both his parents and the grandparents who helped raise him—come from a different American tradition. Looking for a fresh start, more than once, they reinvented themselves with changes of careers and moves to new places. Barack's Kenyan father came to America looking for new opportunities. His mother and grandparents followed the centuries-old pattern of moving west for a second or third chance. They moved from Kansas to Washington State and then to Hawaii, where Barack was born.

The fresh start America offers is special, and it's always a thrill when a dream is fulfilled in an instant. But Michelle's story, with its close ties to the country's past, shows the virtue of keeping a dream alive for as long as it takes.

1

A FAMILY AFFAIR

Chicago, 1968: Four-year-old Michelle La-Vaughn Robinson is trying hard to make her mother, Marian, know she doesn't want attention. She's holding a book that her mother wants to use to teach her to read. Michelle doesn't want help. She's going to teach herself. Michelle's brother, Craig, who is two years older, has been reading on his own since he was Michelle's age. If he can do it, she can. She'll show everyone.

It doesn't happen that way in the end. Marian Robinson teaches Michelle to read. But the pattern is set. Michelle is going to work her way up to the standards she sees around her.

Keeping up with Craig is already a challenge. He's about to skip the second grade. Eventually, as their mother put it, he'll be able to "pass a test just by carrying a book under his arm." Watching Craig makes Michelle want to be "as good or better."

In time, Michelle's instinct about reading like Craig will carry over into athletics, card games, checkers, Monopoly, and, naturally, school. But the two Robinson children are friendly rivals. They stay up in the night talking. They play together, and Craig looks out for Michelle. Years later, in a speech on national television, she will call him "my mentor, my protector, and my lifelong friend."

At crucial moments in each of their lives, the other one will help with advice or an example to follow: a choice about colleges, for example, or advice about a frightening decision to leave a comfortable life for something more meaningful. "She might seem intimidating at first because she's so smart," Craig says, "but my sister is a very warm and sympathetic person.

When the chips are down, she and my wife are the people I talk to."

Michelle and Craig get along better than most siblings for a few simple reasons—to start, their parents won't tolerate anything less, and they are both likable—as well as some reasons that aren't so obvious. During the presidential campaign, Craig Robinson told reporters that to understand Michelle they needed to know about their father, Fraser Robinson III. He could have been speaking about himself too. Fraser Robinson's life shaped his children's personalities in ways that had a lot to do with Michelle's progress to the White House.

DREAMS OF HER FATHER

It's a cool October day in Chicago in the early 1970s. Michelle Robinson, still in grade school, is holding her father's hand as he knocks on a neighbor's door. While they wait, her father steadies himself with his cane. Fraser Robinson III is a big man, and strong—he was a talented boxer and swimmer—but he has multiple sclerosis. It appeared when he was thirty, just a year or so after Michelle was born. Over the course of many years, the disease will leave him unable to walk more than a short distance. He'll trade in the cane for a pair of crutches, and sometimes use a motorized cart.

Michelle adores her father. She idolizes him. She also worries about him.

The neighbor answers the door and lets Michelle and her father inside. Fraser helps Michelle take off her scarf and gloves. They may be staying a while. But this isn't a social visit. Fraser is here to work. He's a precinct captain for the Democratic Party in Chicago, and an election is coming. This neighbor just moved. She isn't registered to vote.

More than thirty years later, as Election Day 2008 came near, it was perfectly natural for Michelle, now Michelle Robinson Obama, to think about this moment with her father. About a week before the election, she shared his example to convince Americans to get to the polls. "Some of my earliest memories," she told a radio audience, "are of tagging along with him as we'd walk door to door and help folks register to vote. We'd sit in neighbors' kitchens for hours and listen to their opinions, their concerns, and the dreams they had for their children. And before we left those kitchens, my father would make sure that everyone could get to the voting booth on Election Day—because he knew that a single vote could help make their dreams a reality."

Michelle's father knew a single vote could *help*, but he was careful not to dream too much. He understood the reality of Chicago politics in the 1960s. He knew the Democratic political machine in Chicago wanted to give the residents of his neighborhood just enough attention to win their votes. Sometimes that attention amounted to nothing more than a holiday turkey. Residents had to push for services that wealthier neighborhoods received.

Fraser was an unlikely player in Chicago politics. To start, he didn't like politicians. He didn't trust them. He passed this feeling on to both Michelle and Craig. Michelle was unsure about Barack's desire to run for office, she later said, "because [politics] seems like a dirty business, and Barack is such a nice guy. I thought, *Eventually he'll come to his senses*." For a long time, Barack referred to Michelle as a "reluctant participant" in his political career. "I generally have shielded her from most of my campaigns," he said before the run for president.

For Fraser, politics came along with his job. He worked the afternoon-to-midnight shift at a city water filtration plant, where he steadily moved up from the boiler room to pump operator to manager. In other cities, the positions he held might have been open to anyone, but in Chicago nearly every city job was handed out as a political favor. Mayor Richard J. Daley, who would run the city for twenty-one years, from 1955 until his death in 1976, made sure that every favor granted led to something in return. For him, politics was not about big ideas. So Fraser Robinson, who worked for the city, put in his time for the Daley machine. The result, Craig Robinson later said, was that "we as a family were extremely cynical about politics and politicians."

Fraser was focused on his family rather than his career. Anyone he met would hear about Michelle and Craig. He was so proud of them that even Marian, who shared his feelings, could be embarrassed. "People ask me about my kids now," she said during Barack's presidential campaign, "and I say I am very proud, but I had to stop talking about them for a long time because my husband bragged about them so much."

Now it's the children who brag about the parent, and with just as much reason. "My dad was our rock," Michelle said in her speech at the 2008 Democratic National Convention, repeating something she had said many times during the campaign. "He was our champion, our hero."

A longtime neighbor remembers Fraser "always had a smile on his face," and was "always joking" despite his challenges. Michelle and Craig, however, knew the difficulties their father faced. Michelle explained, "Seeing a parent with a disability moving through the world and living life as if that disability didn't matter, always made us think, *What do we have to complain about? We wake up, we bound out of bed, we are healthy, we're happy, and our father is struggling to get out of bed.* But he never missed a day of work, never talked about being sick. So it made it hard to wake up and say, 'I don't want to go to school.'"

There are a few kinds of multiple sclerosis. Although one kind has periods in which the disease seems to go away, Fraser had a kind that did not. All types of multiple sclerosis become more severe as time passes. Michelle and Craig saw this happen to their father. They also saw his reaction. "As he got sicker," Michelle told the convention, "it got harder for him to walk. It took him longer to get dressed in the morning. But if he was in pain, he never let on. He never stopped smiling and laughing, even while struggling to button his shirt, even while using two canes to get himself across the room to give my mom a kiss. He just woke up a little earlier and he worked a little harder." The lesson from her father that Michelle stresses most often is, "He didn't complain—ever. He put his energy into us." But there were other more subtle lessons too.

"SHE NEVER TAKES A PASS"

Michelle remembers watching her teenage brother practicing how he would rescue their father from their upstairs apartment in case of a fire. Craig's worries didn't end there. In case something happened to his right hand, he practiced writing with his left. He practiced walking around the house blindfolded, in case he lost his eye-sight. He was "one of those people," Michelle remembered, "who are always preparing for an impending disaster."

Behind all these worries was Fraser's illness. Multiple sclerosis is a mysterious disease: It can lead to a variety of symptoms. They may appear at any time.

The last thing their father wanted was for his children to feel responsible for him, but he didn't have a choice. He and Marian taught Michelle and Craig about responsibility. He had to live with the consequences.

Michelle also learned from the uncertainty of her father's illness. "When you have a parent with a disability," Michelle explained to reporter Holly Yeager, "control and structure become critical habits, just to get through the day." Even now, Michelle stays extraordinarily well organized. It has become second nature. It's how she puts off worry, just like when the worry was her father. "She never takes a pass," says her close friend and former boss Valerie Jarrett, who has become an adviser to Barack. "Even after Barack announced [his candidacy for the U.S. Senate], she'd come to every meeting overprepared. You never would have known what was going on in her life."

Fraser's illness led both Michelle and Craig to put a lot of pressure on themselves from an early age. Because of their father's courage, Michelle said, "You never wanted to disappoint him." It didn't matter that Fraser wielded his moral authority with a light touch, mostly just giving his children a look that said what he was thinking. They knew. "If he was disappointed in you, it was the worst thing that could happen in your life," Craig remembered.

That's a lot for a kid to handle. It's natural for kids to disappoint their parents sometimes. It's part of learning and growing up. Michelle and her brother, however, didn't grow up feeling they could make the same mistakes most other kids make. "We always felt we couldn't let Dad down because he worked so hard for us," Craig says. "My sister and I, if one of us ever got in trouble with my father, we'd both be crying. We'd both be like, 'Oh, my god, Dad's upset. How could we do this to him?'"

It wasn't a question they had to ask themselves often. "I always say Michelle raised herself from about nine years old," Marian Robinson says. "She had her head on straight very early." In her own way, Michelle was doing what she saw as her part. Her father and mother had enough to worry about without worrying about her too.

"THE GREATEST GIFT"

Despite Fraser's illness, the mood at the Robinson home was light. Barack would later say the Robinsons were like the family on the *Leave It to Beaver* television show: a cheerful dad, a mom who made lunches and listened to the kids talk about school, and kids who never got into serious trouble.

As an adult, Michelle remembered her childhood just as her parents hoped. "It was the greatest gift a child could receive," she said about the way Marian and Fraser raised her, "never doubting for a single minute that you're loved and cherished and have a place in this world."

Fraser and Marian put up a partition to turn their living room into two bedrooms, one each for Michelle and Craig. According to one of Michelle's friends, the result was "the smallest room I had ever seen. It was like a closet." But in true 1960s style, Michelle equipped it with a doll house and an Easy-Bake oven, and there was room to play with her African American Barbie, Christie, and Ken.

As for actual television, only one hour a night was allowed. But "somehow," her brother said, "she has managed to commit to memory every single episode of *The Brady Bunch*." Michelle and Craig both liked reading, and their mother kept them challenged with books that were ahead of what teachers expected them to read.

Downstairs in the two-story building was a separate apartment where one of Michelle's great-aunts lived. She was a piano teacher. Michelle took lessons from her. If ever there was a clue that Fraser and Marian had drawn lucky cards with their children, it was this: Michelle practiced without being pushed.

The house was on a street that ran just one block, so it had very little traffic. There was a park at one end. That meant plenty of room to play outside. When they were young, both Michelle and Craig were athletic. But as her brother began to excel in organized sports, Michelle turned her focus elsewhere. There was only so much following she would do, especially given the difficulty of matching Craig. From an early age, he showed the promise that led him to play professional basketball.

Fraser and Marian made it a point to let Michelle and Craig speak their minds, and to question authority. Marian remembered, "We told them, 'Make sure you respect your teachers, but don't hesitate to question them. Don't even allow us to just say anything to you. Ask us why.'" They did. A lot.

In Michelle's case, it's just as well that they didn't try to stop her. That probably would have been impossible. As soon as she could speak, she said what was on her mind, especially if she thought something was wrong. Her mother liked that. Marian didn't have that freedom when she was growing up. "I always resented it when I couldn't say what I felt," she remembered about her childhood. "I always felt like, 'What was wrong with me saying what I feel?'"

Michelle's elementary school, Bryn Mawr (now known as Bouchet Math and Science Academy), was around the corner from her house. By the time she enrolled in first grade, some of the teachers knew from Craig's example what they'd get from Michelle:

a curious and demanding mind. However, it took Michelle a while to understand that Marian's relaxed attitude about kids speaking their minds wasn't shared by every teacher. If Michelle saw something she didn't think was right, she said so. If the teacher didn't respond as thoughtfully as Michelle expected—thanks to her parents' example—Michelle could lose her temper. One time a teacher complained to Marian, who just laughed. "Yeah, she's got a temper," Marian said. "But we decided to keep her anyway!"

What made Michelle angry, even then, was the difference between what she knew from home and what she saw in school. Craig remembered one of the lessons their father tried to pass on: "Life's not fair. It's not. And you don't always get what you deserve, but you have to work hard to get what you want. And then sometimes you don't get it; even if you work hard and do all the right things, you don't get it." All of that is true, and it's worth saying. But life was fair for Michelle at home, thanks to Fraser and Marian and Craig. So it wasn't easy for Michelle to understand why life shouldn't be fair everywhere.

Craig remembers how young Michelle saw the world: "When we were young kids, our parents divided the bedroom we shared so we could each have our own room. Many nights we would talk when we were supposed to be sleeping. My sister always talked about who was getting picked on at school or who was having a tough time at home. I didn't realize it then, but I realize it now: Those were the people she was going to dedicate her life to, the people who were struggling with life's challenges."

MOTHER KNOWS BEST

Even in elementary school, Fraser and Marian challenged Michelle. Marian was determined to keep Michelle ahead of teachers' expectations. Teaching Michelle to read at an early age was just the start. Fraser and Marian, who had both skipped second grade, made sure Craig and Michelle did the same. "If you aren't challenged, you don't make any progress," Marian later explained. Marian also brought home workbooks for Michelle and Craig, who learned early that good enough wasn't good enough.

Marian, like her husband and children, has a strong

competitive streak. (After winning gold medals in sprinting in the Illinois Senior Olympics a few years after Michelle and Craig left for college, an injury slowed her down and she dropped out of racing. "If I can't do it fast, I'm not doing it," she said. "You don't run just to be running—you run to win.") She pushed Michelle and Craig academically as if she were coaching a sport.

"The academic part came first and early in our house," said Craig. "Our parents emphasized hard work and doing your best. Once you get trained like that, then you get used to it and you don't want to get anything but As and Bs."

Like a good coach, Marian pushed Michelle into new and challenging experiences. The school's program for advanced students began in the sixth grade, and Michelle was in it for the next three years, until graduation. She began studying French three years before most students were offered it in ninth grade. She took biology classes at Kennedy-King College.

Kennedy-King exposed her to more than just the inside of frogs. The college was almost four miles away from Bryn Mawr. Earlier than most of her classmates, Michelle was taking independent steps toward her education, searching it out rather than expecting it to come to her. The confidence she gained would soon lead her in unexpected directions.

But first, graduation: Michelle finished Bryn Mawr second in her class of more than one hundred students.

2

THE ROOTS

From when she was about ten years old, Michelle and her family made summertime visits to her grandparents in South Carolina. Fraser's father had been born there, and after retiring from work he and Fraser's mother moved back to his old hometown, a city on the coast, Georgetown. As Michelle and her family came to the end of their long drives from Chicago, the road would become flat and the fields alongside it would start to give off a marshy smell. This part of the South Carolina is known as "lowcountry," because a lot of the land is below sea level, leaving it soggy or flooded for most of the year.

When Michelle started to visit, she discovered she had many relatives in the area. Aunts, uncles, and cousins seemed to be all over Georgetown. But it wasn't until many years later, when Barack's campaign attracted the attention of reporters, that some of the most interesting details of the Robinson family's history began to emerge. The lowcountry marshes of South Carolina were once a center of America's economy and culture. The deep roots of Michelle's achievements are here.

ALL SAINTS

In the story of American slavery, Georgetown stands out. The fields in this area were home to several of the country's largest slave plantations.

The largest slave owner in the United States was Joshua J. Ward of Georgetown. By the start of the Civil War in 1861, he owned 1,130 slaves. At the time, an average slave owner in South Carolina owned fifteen slaves. The average in other states was lower. Across the country, only one owner in a hundred owned more than two hundred slaves.

Ward's neighbors included Robert Allston, who owned 631 slaves and was part of an extended family that owned several thousand, and J. Harleston Read, who owned 511 slaves.

The smallest plantation in the area around Georgetown (then known as All Saints Parish and now Georgetown County) had ninety slaves. The average had almost three hundred. These figures are several times more than the average found on farms and plantations in the rest of the country.

Why were there so many more slaves on the local plantations? Because of the crop that was grown there, rice. It requires many more workers than tobacco or cotton does. One hundred slaves might need as long as fifteen years to make an entire plantation ready. Rice grows best in flooded fields, so the slaves had to build a complex network of ditches and canals that could trap and release water according to the growing schedule. "It was back-breaking work," according to Pat Doyle, president of the Georgetown County Historical Society. "You had to clear the marsh, get the stumps up and put in dikes before you ever planted the first grain of rice."

It was also deadly. The swampy fields were home to alligators and poisonous snakes. The standing water bred mosquitoes that spread malaria and yellow fever. Those diseases claimed many lives. "In the summers," writes historian William Dusinberre, "well-to-do people deserted Georgetown like the plague." The plantation owners "would no more have thought of passing a summer in Georgetown than of making a voluntary sojourn in Hades."

The intricate rice fields had to be tended constantly. The soil became muck and had to be cleared out of the ditches. Then the rice had to be harvested, which was a chore in itself. Rice is a heavy crop.

However, at the time, rice was a cash bonanza. The British government's rules about importing goods worked to the benefit of the Georgetown planters, who produced almost half of the rice grown in the United States. "No region offered such fabulous fortunes," writes historian William Freehling. Before the Revolutionary War, the owners of Georgetown's plantations were "perhaps America's richest entrepreneurs."

The slave community that created this wealth was also special. It was better able to preserve African traditions because it was more isolated from whites than most slave communities were. In all, more than eighty-five percent of the people living in All Saints Parish were African American—the highest percentage in the country. During the malaria season, when whites left the area, that number rose to ninety-eight percent. One local planter wrote, "I am actually so startled at the sight of a white face that I avoid my own...in the [mirror] in the morning."

The result of this separation was a special culture that came to be called Gullah. Its sources were the rice-producing regions of Africa, such as Senegal, Gambia, and Sierra Leone. Slave traders called this the "rice coast." The Georgetown plantation owners strongly preferred slaves from this region. Many of these Africans were already resistant to malaria. They arrived in South Carolina with a knowledge of rice farming. Gullah is a mix of the cultures brought to America. For example, although the Gullah language is based on English, it borrows many of its words and much of its grammar from African languages.

At one time, Gullah culture could be found from

North Carolina to Florida. Its heart, however, was in All Saints Parish. (It's still a strong presence in South Carolina and Georgia.) Historian Charles Joyner has called All Saints Parish "a seedbed of black culture in the United States." That also makes it a seedbed of American culture in general. Just one example: When kindergarten students learn the song "Michael, Row the Boat Ashore," they're singing a Gullah hymn. This self-reliant community is where the American era of Michelle's family story begins.

On summer vacations, young Michelle and her family drove into Georgetown on a highway that became the city's Highmarket Street. This road once connected some of the rice plantations to the downtown port section of Georgetown. Cruising along, none of the Robinsons ever noticed an unmarked dirt side road, about five miles from downtown, that disappeared into a forest of large oak trees. This road led to Friendfield, the old rice plantation where Michelle's great-great-grandfather, Jim Robinson, was a slave.

FRIENDFIELD

Friendfield still exists, though it's no longer a working rice farm. Now the overgrown paddies give it the look of a nature preserve. But many of the old canals dug by slaves remain. More astonishing, some of the old slave cabins are still there too. Small, simple buildings of plain boards, they now seem to be far removed from the owner's house. Once, however, these cabins were the most important buildings on the property, and the people who lived here knew that nothing got done at Friendfield unless they did it.

When Jim Robinson was born, around 1850, Friendfield was already a century old. James Withers, the son of the original owner, had just died a few years before. Born before the Revolutionary War, Withers had collected a huge fortune from the plantation. The rice harvested by the Friendfield slaves allowed him to buy land throughout the area and to make generous cash gifts to his family.

Withers built Friendfield's "big house," as the owners' mansions were called. It immediately became one of most admired homes in the state when it was built in 1818. The governor of South Carolina came to the celebration to mark its completion. Although it burned down to its foundations in 1926, it is still considered historically important. Photographs taken of the interiors before the fire appear in art books. (The house was later rebuilt using the original floor plan, then finished with decorations taken from a nearby house of the same era.)

There was nothing modest about the house, which was meant to display Withers's wealth. It could have stood as the model for Scarlett O'Hara's home in *Gone With the Wind*. The wrought-iron porch railings were intricate. A wide circular staircase ran from the entry room to the second and third floors. The ceilings in its large rooms were thirteen feet tall. The windows, also oversized, were covered by curtains of red velvet. The house had a large library, of course. Many if not most of the books would have been imported from Great Britain. The doorknobs were imported ceramic and sterling silver rather than local iron. The living room had a large marble fireplace and careful paneling.

From the time the house was first built, through Michelle's great-great-grandfather's life, and into the twentieth century, the house had another distinctive decoration for which it's still known today: hand-painted scenic wallpaper from France. All the house's owners were proud of it. Created by a prestigious firm, the wallpaper showed the important monuments of Paris, such as Notre Dame Cathedral and the Luxembourg Palace. (The Eiffel Tower was a few decades in the future.) The paper was eight-and-a-half feet tall and forty-eight feet from end to end. Two hundred and fifty artists worked on it. From a modern perspective, it may seem like an unusual way to display wealth and good taste, but it was the height of style when Friendfield was built. Some of the most notable houses of that period were decorated with similar designs. A set of the same scene from another home of Friendfield's era is on permanent display at the Metropolitan Museum of Art in New York City. The best examples are found in another famous home from that period, also built by slaves: the White House.

One more detail about Friendfield is worth mentioning. The slaves who dug canals in the rice fields then did the same near the big house. In the late 1700s or early 1800s the plantation owners decided they wanted a large water garden, with canals that snaked around small islands planted with flowers and exotic trees. The slaves made it large enough, and dug the canals deep enough, so that a flat-bottomed boat could be paddled around the islands.

MEET THE ROBINSONS

I t's not known how Michelle's great-great-grandfather Jim Robinson came to Friendfield. He might have been born there, or he might have come as a child. But he did live at Friendfield as a slave, and, after the Civil War, as a free man.

His last name, which he eventually passed on to Michelle, isn't much help. It's difficult to trace because "Robinson" was the name of several slave owners. There's a slave cemetery at Friendfield, but the few markers show only the slaves' first names. (Two more unmarked slave cemeteries are up the coast in Myrtle Beach, South Carolina, where the family cemetery of Fairfield's original owners is located.) Also, some government records spell his name differently.

In 1860, just before the Civil War began, there were 273 slaves at Friendfield. Many stayed in the area after the Union's victory freed them. Some continued to work on the plantation. The family history passed down through the years isn't certain, but it seems that Jim Robinson was one of those workers. In government records from 1880, he's listed as a farmer. He might have been hired help, or he might have farmed a section of the plantation and paid for the land by giving the owner a share of the crop.

Michelle is descended from Jim Robinson's third son. Like her own father, he was named Fraser. He was born in 1884, almost twenty years after freedom came to the slaves of South Carolina.

In common with most children of the time, Fraser was illiterate. South Carolina no longer had laws that prevented slaves from learning to read or write, but the state's African American children were still expected to work rather than go to school. There were exceptions, of course: Claflin University, Benedict College, and Allen University had already been founded. Historian Charles Joyner quotes a former slave, Ben Horry, who understood the power of early literacy for each new generation of African

Americans: "You had the learning in your head. Give me that pencil to catch up!" However, for a child like Fraser, education wasn't assumed. Then when he was ten years old something happened to change his life.

He was in the brush near his home, collecting firewood, when a tree fell the wrong way and broke his arm. According to family history, his stepmother didn't think the wound was serious, and didn't treat it properly. The wound then became badly infected. (This version may have been influenced by ten-year-old Fraser's feelings about his stepmother. They didn't get along. Maybe the wound became infected simply because Fraser was a young boy living in a swampy, rural area, and he didn't keep his arm clean.) The infection threatened to spread, which could have killed Fraser. A decision was made. His left arm was amputated.

Despite the tragedy, Fraser's spirits bounced back. His attitude would have been familiar to Michelle: It was the same attitude Fraser's grandson, her father, had about multiple sclerosis. Never complain about it. Never give in to it. Another family legacy.

A neighbor, Frank Nesmith, took notice of the young man. Fraser made himself Nesmith's sidekick.

In time, Nesmith asked Fraser's father, Jim, if Fraser could move in with the Nesmith family. It would give everyone a break from the conflicts between Fraser and his stepmother. Nesmith promised to take care of Fraser. Jim Robinson agreed.

Nesmith, about thirty years old, was married and had a young daughter. Government records from just a few years later, 1900, show the family living in downtown Georgetown. There were two Nesmith girls then, ages seven and one. Nesmith's occupation was listed as train conductor. Fraser, age sixteen, was listed as "house boy." (His last name was listed as "Roberson," as it would be in some government records for the next thirty years.) He still had not learned to read and write, but that would soon change.

Over the next decade, three more Nesmith girls would arrive, and all of them would attend school. Fraser noticed that Frank and his wife took school seriously. "They pushed their kids hard into education," Fraser's niece Carrie Nelson told *Washington Post* reporter Shailagh Murray. "One day Uncle Fraser would, too, because that's what he learned from them." Just as important: He taught himself to read and write. Mrs. Nesmith, probably helped him, but according to family history he mostly learned on his own. That's not easy to do, as four-year-old Michelle would discover many years later.

Fraser also took on new work—a lot of it. He had three jobs. One was at a lumber mill where Frank Nesmith had gone to work after leaving the railroad. The fast-growing Atlantic Coast Lumber Company had become the town's biggest employer, because few people were willing to work in the rice fields anymore. Fraser worked with the mill's kiln, the large oven where freshly cut boards were dried. He was also a shoemaker, and he sold newspapers on a street corner in Georgetown. One longtime resident of the city, Dorothy Taylor, told the *Washington Post* she remembered seeing him there when she was a student. For some reason, she knew that he always took his spare copies home and made sure his children read them—just like Michelle's mother brought home extra workbooks to keep Michelle and Craig ahead of their classes fifty years later.

Fraser's children included a son named Fraser Jr. This is Michelle's grandfather—the one she has come to South Carolina to visit. Fraser Jr. was the oldest of nine children. Government records from 1930 show that the five oldest, ranging from seventeen-year-old Fraser to a seven-year-old brother, had all absorbed Fraser Sr.'s lessons about education and could read and write. Only the infants in the family couldn't.

By the time Fraser Jr. was in his teens, his father had created a comfortable life for the large family. Fraser Jr. had done his part by excelling in school. He didn't go to college, however. By 1930, when he was eighteen, he was working in the lumber yard. The company now claimed to be the largest of its kind in the world, and it might have been. Its enormous factory produced hundreds of thousands of feet of boards a day, and its warehouse held millions of feet of lumber ready for shipment from the huge docks the company had built at Georgetown's port. It was one reason Fraser Sr. had been able to build a large home. Other family members, like Fraser Sr.'s brother, Gabriel, had also become comfortable thanks to work related to the lumber yard. Gabriel had bought a farm with his earnings. Fraser Jr. imagined the same success for himself. So he went to work.

Then the Great Depression began. By 1932, the Atlantic Coast Lumber Company was out of business.

THE GREAT MIGRATION

Losing a job is bad enough, but for African Americans the Depression became dangerous in other ways. Racial violence had already increased during the previous few decades. It was now extreme.

The problem had begun about a dozen years after the Civil War ended. At the time, the former Confederate states were still under the legal control of the national government in Washington, D.C., which put the U.S. Army in charge. In a way, the southern states were being treated as if they had been foreign countries during the war. That was, after all, exactly how they had asked to be treated before they lost the war. The goal of Reconstruction, as the federal government's plan was called, was to set rules that the states could follow in order to govern themselves again and have a voice in Congress. These rules included protections for the rights of African Americans, such as the right to vote.

Reconstruction was strongly opposed in the South. The country's most notorious hate group, the Ku Klux Klan, was formed at this time. It was one of many white supremacy groups that sought to terrorize African Americans. An informal rebellion was taking place. This was a period of great violence against African Americans and whites who supported Reconstruction. Then Reconstruction suddenly ended, thanks to a political deal.

After the votes were counted in the 1876 presidential election, both the Democrats and the Republicans claimed victory. For several months, legal fights and political arguments dragged on. At the last minute, a deal was struck to give the presidency to the Republican candidate, Rutherford B. Hayes, whose support came from the North. In return, the former Confederate states, who had backed the Democratic candidate, got what they wanted in the first place: An agreement to end Reconstruction.

Soon old faces were back in power in the South. They immediately passed laws to take from African Americans the rights that were granted during Reconstruction. Voting rights were the first to go. They created elaborate rules designed specifically to exclude African Americans. Then they passed laws requiring segregation. In South Carolina, for example, it was illegal for a restaurant to serve whites and African Americans in the same room, even if the owner wanted to do so. These segregation laws were called "Jim Crow" laws, after an African American character in a music hall song.

The lowest moment in the history of Jim Crow may have come in 1913, when President Woodrow Wilson and members of his cabinet introduced segregation in the federal government. This ranged from building crude office partitions to the firing of African American employees. Just a little later in Michelle's story, another connection between her life and the turning points of American history will appear when becomes part of Woodrow Wilson's most cherished legacy, a university built on the same beliefs he brought to the presidency.

Voting rules and Jim Crow laws would be the target of the civil rights movement in the 1960s, but that was still a long way off for young men like Michelle's grandfather. In the decade or so before the lumber yard closed, attacks on African Americans had become extreme. African Americans who had served in World War I came home in 1919 imagining that new opportunities waited for them. They found a fresh wave of Ku Klux Klan members who feared successful African Americans and were ready to do violence. The KKK and other groups and mobs even killed African American soldiers in uniform. The summer of 1919 is called "Red Summer" because so many riots against African Americans broke out. The first one happened in Charleston, South Carolina, not far from Georgetown.

The lack of work, Jim Crow, violence: Michelle's grandfather decided he'd had enough. He did what more than a million southerners had done in the decade and a half or so since the beginning of World War I. He moved north.

This was the tail end of what's now called the Great Migration. African Americans from the southern states moved to the cities of the North, often switching from jobs in farming to work in factories. The African American population of major northern cities boomed.

Michelle's grandfather chose Chicago, where the family would stay until Michelle and Barack moved into the White House. By the time he arrived, the African American community had already ballooned to more than five times the size it had been in 1910. It was growing at ten times the rate of the city's overall growth. About one of every five new residents was African American. A quarter of a million African Americans lived in Chicago by the time Fraser Jr. arrived.

A lot of them were looking for work. Michelle's grandfather eventually got a job at the post office. He met and married a Chicago native, LaVaughn Johnson, whose parents had moved to the city from Mississippi many years before. Michelle's middle name comes from this grandmother.

Fraser Jr.'s dreams of success in Chicago didn't work out as he'd hoped, probably because of the timing of his move. The Depression hit hard. Then, after World War II, another wave of African Americans moved north—what historians call the Second Great Migration. Competiton for jobs was tough. More than that, he discovered segregation and racism in Chicago too. Regulations made it unusually difficult for African American families to freely choose where to live. Fraser Jr. and his wife ended up in one of the public housing projects that were within an accepted area. This bothered Fraser. "He was a very proud man. He was proud of lineage," Michelle told the *Washington Post*. "There was a discontent about him." Her grandfather remembered his childhood in South Carolina fondly and talked about it often. After leaving his job at the post office, Fraser Jr. didn't waste time before moving south. He and Michelle's grandmother joined the same church, Bethel AME, where his family had been worshiping since before he was born. They became active in the Georgetown community.

That's when Michelle's childhood trips to South Carolina began. Of course, she was a city girl. The loud and unfamiliar chirping of crickets kept her awake. She didn't like some of the food. But she met and came to know relatives she'd only heard about, and some she didn't know existed. She still has a lot of family in Georgetown.

OTHER BRANCHES

Some of Michelle's southern connections haven't been discovered yet. The story of her mother's side of the family is also not as clear as the story of her father's side. That's part of the African American experience too. Slave owners broke family ties. Slaves didn't leave the trail of official documents—land purchase contracts, for example, or wills—that historians usually follow. Because in many places slaves weren't allowed to read and write, they didn't leave personal letters behind.

For instance, not much is known yet about Michelle's great-great-grandmother, Rosa Ellen Cohen, who was Fraser Jr.'s wife. She seems to be a descendant of one of the European families who moved to Georgetown in the late 1700s. There were a few branches of a family named Cohen, a Jewish family that may have come from Portugal. A modern descendant of the Cohens, Sadie Pasha, who has researched the family for many years, says at least one Cohen in Georgetown passed along his name to mixed-race children in the early 1800s.

Without more evidence, we can't know the exact relationship that led to this branch of Michelle's family tree. There are at least a few possibilities.

There's a small chance that Michelle is descended from a free African American woman who worked for one of the Cohen families and came to be known by the family name. Government records from early 1800s show 930 African Americans living in

Georgetown, of whom eighty were free citizens. It's also known that some of the Jewish people in South Carolina had children with Native Americans. One of these children may have then formed a family with an African American woman and given her his name. But these aren't the most likely possibilities.

Some of the Cohens owned slaves. Rosa Ellen was likely descended from a relationship between slave and owner. Michelle and the rest of her family believe there is at least one slave owner in her family tree.

This subject isn't spoken about openly in every family. It leads to uncomfortable questions that are difficult to answer: Would the slave have chosen this relationship? Was the slave too frightened to refuse? Even if the relationship had been a loving one, those partnerships were never equal: If trouble arose, one partner had legal rights and the other had none. But a belief about a slave owner in the family isn't passed down lightly, even if it's passed down by whispers.

Michelle, as usual, is open and direct about this. As she explained to the *Washington Post*, "A lot of times these stories get buried, because sometimes the pain of them makes it hard to want to remember," she said. "You've got to be able to acknowledge and understand the past and move on from it. You have to understand it, and I think a lot of us just don't have an opportunity to understand it. But it's there." Barack stated the family belief directly in his speech about race in America, "A More Perfect Union," given during the 2008 primary campaign: "I am married to a black American who carries within her the blood of slaves and slave owners."

If we do eventually confirm that Michelle has such an ancestor, as we probably will, we may still be surprised by the full story. Some of these relationships were more complicated than they first appear. Because the slavery laws in South Carolina made it almost impossible for some owners to free their slaves, some free citizens were married in every way but legally to spouses who were, by law, still slaves. But stories like these are exceptions.

Michelle is focused on the positive. "An important message in this journey is that we're all linked," Michelle told the *Post*. "Somewhere there was a slave owner—or a white family in my great-grandfather's time that gave him a place, a home, that helped him build a life—that again led to me. So who were those people? I would argue they're just as much a part of my history as my great-grandfather."

Her family story, she said, is like many others. "There are probably thousands of one-armed Frasers, all over this country, who, out of slavery and emancipation, because they were smart and worked hard, those American values, were able to lift themselves up." Yet when she finally learned the story as an adult, it also explained to her a lot about her own life. "It makes more sense to me," she said, "if the patriarch in our lineage was one-armed Fraser, a shoemaker with one arm, an entrepreneur, someone who was able to own property, and with sheer effort and determination was able to build a life in this town. That must have been the messages that my grandfather got."

She could have added: And what he passed down.

3

CLASS ACT

September, 1977: Michelle's first day of high school. This isn't just around the corner, like Bryn Mawr elementary. Michelle's not going to the local high school. To get here, she has traveled an hour and a half on two city buses. Now the thirteen-year-old is in a part of the Chicago that seems to have more warehouses than homes.

She chose this for herself. Her brother isn't going to the local high school, so why should she?

Craig attended Mount Carmel, a private boys' school. It was smaller than the local school, and tougher academically. It also had a great sports program. NFL star Donovan McNabb attended Mount Carmel in the 1990s, helping the team win a state championship. Antoine Walker of the NBA is another graduate. It was the perfect school for Michelle's brother. When he wasn't being challenged in the classroom, he was starring on the basketball court.

But when it came to taking on challenges, Michelle had him beat. Her school, Whitney M. Young, was a true adventure.

The distance from home was one reason. But Michelle could handle the daily trips, even though they sometimes added up to three hours. The classes at Kennedy-King College that were part of the gifted program at Bryn Mawr elementary had given her confidence.

Whitney M. Young was also meant to be an experiment for Chicago. It opened just two years before Michelle started ninth grade. It was a magnet school, drawing kids from all over the city. Chicago had long been a collection of ethnic neighborhoods, with boundaries that were invisible but difficult to cross. Whitney M. Young was meant to erase those boundaries, at least for its students. It would be the first time that many of them, Michelle included, were in a class that reflected Chicago's diversity. It was a big step for the city, and for all the students who chose to attend.

However, what really drew Michelle and most of her classmates were the school's superior academics. In addition to taking advanced placement classes, Whitney M. Young students could take college courses at the University of Illinois. In a way, it was like the gifted program at Bryn Mawr. It had no ceiling on the opportunities it offered. That made it perfect for a student who constantly pressured herself to take on new challenges.

Dagny Bloland, a teacher at Whitney M. Young, echoed this in an interview with *Washington Post* reporter and *Michelle* author Liza Mundy: "When [Michelle] applied and came here, the tradition of leaving one's neighborhood to go to high school was very new, and a person had to be very gutsy to do it.

For most of the kids who came here in those times, the idea that you would take two or three buses and a train to come here was a very new idea. . . . It was a real experiment to come here. I think you had to be the sort of person and the sort of family that would put education above everything else."

"Gutsy" might be the perfect word to describe Michelle in high school. It was hard work for her. She was one of those students who do not do well in tests, something she still mentions in speeches. So she made up for it in other ways. Her brother remembered her doing her homework for hours without stopping, while he would rush through his, play basketball, and watch television. But she made the honor roll all four years, and was inducted into the National Honor Society.

By this time, her mother had already stopped pushing her. There was no need. Harriette Cole of *Ebony* magazine asked Marian Robinson, "What would happen if [Michelle] came home with grades that weren't the best grades?" Michelle's mom thought that was pretty funny. "That didn't happen," she said, laughing.

But it almost did. A typing teacher gave Michelle

a B, even though Michelle had scored enough for an A on the scoring scale the teacher had posted for the class. The teacher's reason? She just didn't give As. That was her philosophy. Michelle was furious. That just wasn't right—and Michelle had long before developed a way of dealing with things that just weren't right. "She badgered and badgered that teacher," Michelle's mother remembered with admiration and amusement. "I finally called her and told her, 'Michelle is not going to let this go.'" Michelle got the grade she'd earned.

Another word comes up again and again in interviews with classmates: "focused." Classmate Michelle Ealey Toliver told biographer Liza Mundy, "She didn't goof off like some other students. . . . She was on a very advanced, focused track." (That made her the exact opposite of her future husband. "I was sort of a goof-off," Barack once told his *Chicago Tribune* reporter and biographer David Mendell.)

Both the public that knows Michelle through the media and the family that knows her best would be surprised to learn a few classmates remember Michelle as quiet. This wasn't shyness. It was a no-nonsense attitude about work. But as Barack would one day realize, even before her family did, there was also a more serious element to it. There was some fear. She was still a kid who could see from her father's example that trouble could appear at any moment.

As a result of her quiet focus, classmates say she appeared to accomplish her goals with ease. She seemed to get along with nearly everyone. She had time for activities, like dance. She was student council treasurer. Whitney M. Young was a school where an enthusiastic student like Michelle fit right in. A lot of her classmates were the same. Like Michelle, they had chosen to be part of this experiment. Whitney M. Young wasn't "just a bunch of kids that [came] here from different neighborhoods," Dagny Bloland said. It was "a real shared commitment." Behind the students were supportive parents. As Bloland told Mundy, parents sent their kids to Whitney M. Young thinking, "My child is going to have a wider world."

Race was part of that. Fortunately for the students, it was just as the planners had hoped: no big deal.

The original idea had been that forty percent of the students would be African American, forty percent would be white, ten percent Spanish-speaking,

Polaris

Michelle Robinson Obama in
elementary school and in a high
school dance performance.
Michelle, who was reading before
she entered elementary school,
skipped the second grade. Although
she was also athletic, she chose not
to participate in sports as she grew
up, partly to be different from her
older brother, Craig, who was a star
athlete from a young age.

Courtesy Whitney M. Young High School

Courtesy Whitney M. Young High School

Courtesy Whitney M. Young High School

Polaris

Michelle chose to attend Whitney M. Young High School, a magnet school that was an hour-and-a-half trip from home each day. It was a new school in Chicago, established in part to bring together the city's ethnic groups. TOP: Michelle and other members of the National Honor Society. BOTTOM LEFT: Michelle, who was treasurer of her senior class, with fellow class officers. BOTTOM RIGHT: Graduation from Princeton University, 1985.

OPPOSITE PAGE, TOP: Slave cabins still stand at the former plantation in South Carolina where Michelle's great-great-grandfather Jim Robinson was a slave. OPPOSITE PAGE, CENTER: The owner's mansion. OPPOSITE PAGE, BOTTOM: Jim Robinson's son, Fraser, who was Michelle's great-grandfather, and Fraser's wife, Rosella Cohen Robinson. Born in 1884, Fraser wasn't taught to read or write, but he began the family tradition of emphasizing education for his children.

All photos this page: © Melina Mara/The Washington Post

Polaris

Polaris

Polaris

Polaris

Polaris

OPPOSITE PAGE, CLOCKWISE FROM TOP LEFT: Michelle after graduating from Harvard Law School; Barack and his mother, Ann Dunham; Barack at Harvard Law School in 1990, about the time Michelle met him in Chicago. THIS PAGE, TOP: Michelle and Barack at their wedding reception, October 1992. BOTTOM: The bride and groom with Michelle's mother, Marian, at left, and Barack's mother second from right.

Daughter Malia Ann was born in 1998 and daughter Sasha in 2001. During these years, Michelle was the associate dean of student services for the University of Chicago. She had established the university's first office of community service. Barack was an Illinois state senator. At the time of the photos above, in 2004, he was running for the U.S. Senate. BOTTOM LEFT: Michelle's mother, Marian Robinson, who would be essential in Michelle's plans for Malia and Sasha's care during the 2008 presidential campaign.

© Spencer Platt/Getty Images

ABOVE: In July 2004, while running for the U.S. Senate, Barack, who was practically unknown outside Illinois, was given the opportunity to make the opening speech at the Democratic National Convention. To calm his nerves before he walked onstage, Michelle gave him a short pep talk: "Just don't screw it up, buddy." He didn't, and instantly became a national figure. BELOW: Immediately after the speech.

Polaris

Election night, November 2, 2004. Barack is the new senator from Illinois.

five percent other races, and five percent the choice of the principal. (The politicians who agreed to the school wanted to be able to ask for a favor.) It didn't recruit quite as many white students as the planners had hoped, even though standards were lowered for white students so more of them could get in. But the ones who came were happy to be breaking down the barriers of the city's closed ethnic neighborhoods. Robert Mayfield, president of Michelle's senior class of 1980–1981, remembered, "It was racially diverse, it was ethnically diverse; it had great school spirit. It was pretty new, and it was fantastic."

The school even had a program for deaf and hearing-impaired students at a time when educators debated whether those students should go to regular schools. The ones who went to Whitney M. Young were like Michelle's father and great-grandfather: Unwilling to be sidelined.

From sports to the homecoming court, Michelle's school was, in the all-American words of her classmate Michelle Ealey Toliver, "a melting pot."

Thirty years later, this description of Whitney M. Young might seem common. It could apply to schools all over America. At the time, it was a significant achievement. The struggle to create this opportunity for students like Michelle began at about the time Michelle was born. It had violently fractured Chicago over the course of Michelle's childhood.

WILLIS WAGONS

S chools were one of the most important issues in the civil rights movement in Chicago. A few months before Michelle was born, two hundred thousand Chicago students—about half of the total number in the city's schools—stayed home from classes as a protest against the city's superintendent of schools. Their parents were furious because the schools in African American neighborhoods were overcrowded. Instead of investing in new schools, Superintendent Benjamin Willis offered portable classrooms, which came to be called "Willis Wagons," in school parking lots and empty lots. Then, trying to double the number of students each school could teach, he started two shifts of classes a day. These were cheap, halfhearted responses to the problem. They only created new trouble. The shift system meant that some kids had very different schedules than those of their working parents. The portables were not made for Chicago's frigid winters.

African American students might have been sent to schools in other neighborhoods, which had room. But Chicago's government worked to keep the city segregated. African Americans parents were also blocked from moving to the neighborhoods with better schools. Most real estate agents would not show them homes. If the families did find a home, banks would not lend them money to buy it. If they didn't need a bank, they might find that a law prevented the house from being sold to anyone who wasn't white. As a result, African Americans tended to be stuck in crowded homes and apartment buildings in just a few neighborhoods. Because African Americans couldn't easily leave, landlords took advantage of them. Buildings weren't repaired. Rents were higher than elsewhere in the city.

Breaking these housing barriers wasn't easy. In 1951, an arsonist burnt down three houses that had been sold to African American families, to prevent the families from moving into the white neighborhood. But thanks to hard work by civil rights lawyers and others, a few neighborhoods opened up in the late 1950s and early 1960s. Unfortunately, what happened next was a step backward. As African American families moved in, white families moved out.

Michelle's family saw this happen a few years after they moved into their neighborhood. When Michelle and Craig were young, the neighborhood was mixed. People got along. Then, one by one, the white families left.

Often the reason was just money. Like many families, most of their wealth was in their homes. They feared that as more African Americans moved into the neighborhood, the value of their homes would go down, because no new white families would come. Real estate agents, who wanted to make money from selling the houses, spread this fear. (Selling was often a mistake. Property values went up in some neighborhoods as African Americans moved in.)

Michelle's brother Craig still remembers this: A moving truck in front of a neighbor's house, a car packed with valuables, and the last white family in the neighborhood saying goodbye before leaving Chicago for the suburbs.

In Michelle's neighborhood, the breakdown of old

barriers happened peacefully. But Chicago endured serious riots over this problem. People died. Although Michelle was too young to understand these issues at the time, the conflicts shaped her parents' thoughts, and she absorbed their lessons.

The message to African American parents in Chicago was: The school system does not care about educating your child. It does not believe your child can be educated. This was the same message Michelle's great-grandfather Fraser Sr. had heard in South Carolina at the turn of the century. He rejected it then, and Michelle's parents rejected it too. Fraser Sr. had brought newspapers for his children. Without even knowing that fact, Michelle's parents had the same instinct and brought home workbooks for Michelle and Craig.

The lesson Michelle understood was, opportunities are out there, but you won't reach them unless you cross some boundaries that you may not be supposed to cross. She talked about this when she was back in South Carolina during the 2008 campaign. She was meeting with girls at a community center for kids in public housing. Their lives seemed to be a mix of Michelle's South Carolina roots and Chicago politics. "Does everybody here want to go to college?" she asked. "What do you think it's going to take to get from here to college?" The replies were vague, noted Holly Yeager, a reporter who witnessed the scene. Then Michelle became stern. "You've got to take advantage of every opportunity that comes your way. All right? Trust me, I was right where you guys are. I grew up in the same kind of neighborhood. The thing that made me different from a lot of other kids who didn't have opportunities was that I tried new stuff and I wasn't afraid to be uncomfortable. You guys have got to do that, because the things you want in life will not get handed to you. There is a lot of opportunity out there. But you've got to want it."

Michelle's experience at Whitney M. Young High School was a sign of how far the city had come. The way she grabbed that opportunity was a sign of how far she had come. But the school had not magically erased all of Chicago's old problems and prejudices, or all of Michelle's problems. As she came to the end of high school, she got a shock.

TIGER BEAT

November 1980: Sixteen-year-old Michelle is in the office of one of the school's guidance counselors. She's holding a list of colleges. The applications are complicated, and she wants to be certain she can get all the forms she needs from Whitney M. Young by the December deadline.

Looking at Michelle's file, the counselor asks, "What's your first choice?"

Michelle tells her.

"You can't go there," the counselor says. "Your test scores aren't high enough."

Michelle took that criticism personally, but the real problem was that the advice wasn't personal at all. It was the kind of information that appeared in college guides. The right advice for Michelle would have been to aim high. Especially with Ivy League admissions, which include interviews and personal recommendations from teachers and long applications, a single weakness wasn't fatal.

As it happened, Michelle probably understood Ivy League admissions better than the guidance counselor did. Her brother was in his sophomore year at Princeton University. She had seen colleges compete for him when he was still at Mount Carmel High School. The University of Washington had offered him a full scholarship.

Craig probably would have ended up at Washington, just to save the family the burden of paying for school. He knew that his father had skipped college in part to allow the family to pay tuition for a younger brother. But Craig changed his mind after his father dropped the D-bomb on him: "If you pick a college based on how much I have to pay," his father said, "I'll be very disappointed."

His mother went to work as a secretary at the Spiegel catalog company to help pay for Princeton. She was happy to do it. With her kids practically raised, it was like making time for herself.

Michelle had been delighted for Craig. She looked through all the booklets and bulletins the university sent to incoming students. Envelopes with the school's orange-and-black crest and *P* logo arrived throughout the summer before Craig's first year. Naturally, her friendly competition with him led her to think about the Ivy League for herself. She later remembered, "I knew him, and I knew his study habits, and I was, like, 'I can do that too.'" Or, as she put it on another occasion, "I thought, I'm smarter than him!" She was going to become a Princeton Tiger too.

What the guidance counselor told her only made her more determined. She knew Princeton would look at more than her test scores. She was right. She might not have been perfect on paper, but she was impressive. Princeton's admissions committee also knew from the example of Craig, who was doing well at school and was on his way to becoming one of the college's all-time best athletes, that the Robinson family had a way of exceeding the highest expectations.

In September 1981, she kissed her parents goodbye and headed to college. Hard work had taken her to exactly where she wanted to go, one of the most prestigious universities in the country.

But it wouldn't be long before she was questioning if she had wanted the right thing.

4

ORANGE CRUSH

Stevie Wonder albums. Friends who laughed at her constant wisecracking, and who made her laugh, too. Dancing for any reason at all. Cheering for Craig's amazing performances on the basketball court. The occasional date with a student who wasn't scared off by a big brother hovering around. This was Princeton.

So were problems like this:

Michelle has just met one of her roommates. Their

room is on the top floor of a four-story dormitory, in what was originally an attic. With three beds, three desks, and three dressers, it's packed tightly. Making it feel even more cramped, the angled roof of the building forces the ceiling in this room to slant down toward the floor. The bathroom is downstairs. This is a dormitory with a lot of tradition, which is a polite way of saying it's getting old. But Michelle doesn't care. Everything still seems new to her.

She's sitting on the edge of her bed and talking when her other roommate arrives. The woman seems a little out of breath from carrying two suitcases up the four flights of stairs. Her name's Catherine Rodrigue. She's from New Orleans. While she settles in, Michelle learns about her: She's an athlete, like Craig. Captain of the basketball and volleyball teams at school. Michelle notices from a photo that Catherine was homecoming queen too. As they talk, Michelle starts to sense something familiar about her: Like Michelle, she had to work hard to get here. She was raised by a single mother who took a job at a good school so Catherine, her only child, could attend it. Then her mother, who taught science, tutored Catherine to keep her ahead of her schoolwork.

Catherine's mother, who drove her to Princeton, is waiting at a small hotel near the campus. She and a friend who helped with the driving are going to take Catherine to dinner. Catherine and Michelle say their goodbyes. Not long afterward Michelle finds Craig and they call their parents. Fraser and Marian are only half-listening to the hundred new details of Michelle's life, which are coming out too fast to understand. They just want to hear that Michelle's happy. She is.

But at the hotel where Catherine's mother is staying, the mood is different. Catherine's mother only cares about one detail, and she's furious. Catherine's roommate is *black*? No way. Catherine has to move immediately.

She's so mad she calls her own mother, Catherine's grandmother. Her advice: "Take Catherine out of school right now and bring her home." Catherine's mother spends the evening calling the Princeton alumni back in New Orleans who had helped Catherine apply to the college to get their help.

Catherine already likes Michelle. She thinks Michelle is funny and interesting. But even while they were talking back in the room Catherine expected this problem. Although she's a little embarrassed by her mother's anger, she isn't putting up a fight. She and her mother are close. She doesn't want her mother to be unhappy. She's also used to this behavior.

The next morning her mother enters the housing office like a tank. She doesn't even try to hide her reasons for wanting them to move Catherine. "Catherine is from the South," she told them. "We aren't used to living with black people." Her one effort to be polite is to use the word "black." Normally she uses a word that starts with the letter *n*.

She can't be talked out of her demand. The housing office says it will take some time, but it's possible. Before she leaves, she makes sure the forms are completed. As soon as she gets back to New Orleans, she calls the housing office to push them. She calls again and again over the next months.

"TEMPER AND TRADITION"

To Catherine's credit, Michelle didn't know about the problem at the time. She wouldn't learn until the 2008 campaign, when

Catherine and her mother told the story to the press. By then, both Catherine and her mother had moved on from their old ideas. They were embarrassed, and they were brave enough to be honest about what Catherine said was "her secret shame" at Princeton.

But Catherine and Michelle didn't become close, either. Michelle later wondered to Sally Jacobs of the *Boston Globe* if racism, even if it was just from other members of Catherine's family, might have been the reason. "Sometimes that's the thing you sense, that there's something there, but it's often unspoken."

Catherine did eventually move out. Her mother's efforts led to the offer of a new room that happened to be larger. Catherine said later that she didn't have any bad feelings towards Michelle, she just wanted the extra space. However, there was no effort to remain friends. They didn't even speak when they passed each other on campus, Catherine told the *Globe*.

At the time the story came out, opponents of Barack were saying that Michelle imagined racism that didn't exist, and that she was too quick to complain about it. The incident with Catherine, and her reaction to it, showed the opposite. Often, racism was behind problems that simply puzzled Michelle.

Unfortunately, racism was not rare at Princeton. Lisa F. Rawlings, a classmate of Michelle's, recalled to the *Boston Globe*, "I cannot tell you the number of times I was called 'Brown Sugar.'"

It's likely that the same thing happened at every campus where African Americans were a minority. Princeton, however, might have been worse than some others. It was a school with a long tradition of race problems. Woodrow Wilson, who was president of Princeton before becoming president of the United States, had once said, "The whole temper and tradition of the place are such that no negro has ever applied for admission, and it seems extremely unlikely that the question will ever assume a practical form." In 1936, an African American high school senior who didn't know the school's policy applied and was accepted, but when he showed up he was refused enrollment. Princeton did not admit its first regular African American student until 1947, more than two hundred years after the school was founded.

THE HARD WAY

The people running Princeton in Michelle's time were determined to make up for the school's ugly past. But schools like Princeton don't change direction easily. So although Michelle should have been able to just think about her courses and having fun with friends, she was also stuck in the middle of a nationwide debate about race. After coming from Whitney M. Young High School, where those questions seemed to be in the past, it was a rude shock. It was also insulting.

The debate really came to a simple question: Were African American students really good enough to be at elite schools, or had standards been lowered to let them in?

At Princeton, the critics of minority students were notoriously harsh. A group of alumni was formed to attack the school's policy of encouraging minority enrollment. It came out of a similar group that had fought the admission of women, who first enrolled in 1969. In fact, Princeton was still considered difficult for women of any race when Michelle attended. They faced many of the same attitudes minorities did:

Some of the professors and other university staff believed they were not intelligent enough to understand the work. So Michelle had it doubly hard.

There was something strange about this debate at the Ivy League schools. Some of the alumni who said they were concerned about lower academic standards expected the university to give their own children an advantage for admission. That had been the practice in these schools for generations. A lot of the complaints about Princeton's new policies came from alumni who were worried that there would be fewer places for these "legacies."

Unfortunately, mistaken ideas about lower standards worked against minority students like Michelle. Hilary Beard, who was a year ahead of Michelle at Princeton, told the school's newspaper in 2008 that she still remembered a professor who accused an African American student of copying a paper because the work was very good. "He told her it was not possible that she had this high quality of thinking. [Her work] happened to be brilliant like any other student's on campus, but her skin was brown."

THE CLUB RULES

Having Craig on campus was a help, most of the time. He was already a star player, being tracked by professional teams.

Craig had already gone through the tough transition that many students face when they reach college after going to a high school where teachers push the students and give them attention. In college, a lot of professors are only interested in their own research. They think of teaching as the part of the job they have to endure. They don't give students a lot of direction, but they still expect good work. When Craig first arrived, he remembered, he was "overwhelmed." He was used to breezing his way to the top. But by the time Michelle entered, he was able to give her good advice. One thing was something their father had told him: "You're not going to be number one at Princeton, but not the last either."

Michelle found her balance quickly. As friends remembered, she did more than handle all the course work. She finished it early. She wasn't intimidated by professors, either. One day Craig called his mother to complain. "Mom, Michelle's here telling people they're not teaching French right." Michelle thought the teacher should focus on conversational French rather than literary French. She wanted to be able to communicate with people, not just do academic research. By then, Michelle's mother knew better than to get between Michelle and a teacher. She told Craig, "Just pretend you don't know her."

Michelle also found a way around one of the biggest social perils for African American students at the time, Princeton's "eating clubs." These clubs, unique to Princeton, are a lot like fraternities or sororities. They tend to define the boundaries of a student's social life. The difference is that at Princeton, the official reason for joining is to have a place to take meals, rather than to have a place to live.

Although there are now clubs that choose members at random, joining one of the traditional clubs is like joining a fraternity or sorority. A student might have to endure a lot of interviews, or games, or contests. Then the members decide whether the student is right for the club. In Michelle's time, Princeton's social life was still dominated by the traditional clubs.

Like any club, they weren't just about letting people in; they were also about keeping people out.

Jews were excluded until the 1960s—and later at some clubs. A few clubs excluded women until 1990. The last ones only gave in because of a lawsuit.

Few African American students joined. They "did not feel comfortable in the eating clubs," Hilary Beard remembered. Part of it was the "culture of drunkenness" at some clubs. "In that environment, a lot of things got said to people that might not be said when people were sober, and some of these things were disparaging racial comments."

Michelle didn't try to join a club. The idea behind them didn't fit her personality. She had chosen Princeton because it represented the wider world: new people, new experiences, new opportunities. She was not there to create a narrow, country club life surrounded by people just like her. At Whitney M. Young High School, she had been in a community of students who, like her, wanted to break down barriers. At Princeton, the social life was based on creating walls. Some students had selected the school because of those traditions.

But her rejection of them also showed a less obvious part of her personality. She knew something about Princeton's culture from Craig. She knew it wasn't exactly right for her. But she chose it because of the opportunities it offered, and maybe also because it was something that people would have liked to deny her. She'd later make other choices that people who knew her didn't think were right for her. Although her parents had raised her to do what would make her happy, she was still following traditional ideas about what that was. It would be several years before she would do exactly what she pleased.

Instead of joining an eating club, Michelle joined Stevenson Hall, an alternative student center that had been formed in the late 1960s as part of a student-led movement to open the university to new social and academic ideas. Her roommate, Angela Acree, worked there. It also helped define Michelle's social life, but in ways that would never have happened at a traditional club. Stevenson Hall had a kosher kitchen, because one of its roles was to provide a place to eat for Orthodox Jews, who would never have been admitted to a traditional club in the 1960s. Those students became their friends, Acree recalled to the university newspaper. "[We] did everything the Orthodox students did, which included going on a ski trip to Vermont with them one break."

Michelle also spent a lot of time at the Third World Center, which had been established for minority students. (That name is controversial now. It's thought to imply that the students were poor and poorly edu cated. Some schools with similar student centers still use that name, but Princeton's is now called the Carl A. Fields Center for Equality and Understanding.)

Michelle had a job at the center. She was the coordinator of an after-school child care program for children of Princeton's lunchroom and maintenance staff. Czerny Brasuell, the center's director, was amazed at her ability to bond with the children. Brasuell's son Jonathan, a preschooler, was one. Michelle and Craig became like big sister and big brother to him. The friendships continue to this day. Now in his thirties, Jonathan told the *Boston Globe* he still remembers Michelle thrilling him by playing "Linus and Lucy," the famous jazz piano piece from the "Peanuts" television specials. "I could not go a week without hearing that."

For Michelle, as for many African American students at Princeton, and maybe for most of them, the Third World Center became what the eating clubs were to white students. "The Third World Center was our life," Acree said. "We hung out there, we partied there, we studied there."

BALANCING ACT

Decades later, during the 2008 presidential campaign, opponents of Michelle's and Barack's would feel threatened by how much time Michelle spent at the Third World Center. They would use a paper Michelle wrote in her senior year, "Princeton-Educated Blacks and the Black Community," to fuel fears that Michelle hates white people. That paper, a "senior thesis" of the kind all Princeton undergraduates must complete, would be published on the Internet. Every sentence would be put under a microscope.

What scared the critics was the paper's discussion of the isolation and rejection Michelle experienced at Princeton. "My experiences at Princeton have made me far more aware of my 'Blackness' than ever before," she wrote. "I have found that at Princeton, no matter how liberal and open-minded some of my White professors and classmates try to be toward me,

I sometimes feel like a visitor on campus, as if I really don't belong. Regardless of the circumstances under which I interact with Whites at Princeton, it often seems as if, to them, I will always be Black first and a student second." Michelle wasn't describing how she saw herself; she was describing how she was seen. That was a common experience. It's true Michelle might have overstated the general rule—not every encounter of every African American student put race first. But that may have been Michelle's experience at Princeton. Or it may just be that, as with most senior theses written on a deadline by twenty-one-year-olds, not every word was perfect. Those small questions don't matter. What Michelle wrote about was not something she imagined, which is what Barack's opponents would say decades later.

The more important question, which is at the heart of her thesis, is an old one: Integration or isolation? Every ethnic group faces that question, constantly. Sometimes one side of the debate seems to be in favor, sometimes the other. While Michelle was at Princeton, it was almost impossible for African American students to ignore the question completely. Robin Givhan, a Princeton student at about the same time as Michelle and now a *Washington Post* columnist, told author Liza Mundy she felt pressure to socialize only among African Americans. She felt a little better when her Chinese American roommate told her, "I get that all time from the Chinese kids."

Sometimes the things universities did to help the problem only made the problem worse. Princeton, like Brown and some other schools, invited minority students to campus for Third World Orientation Week to take place before the regular orientation week. Michelle's friend Angela Acree remembered that she and Michelle couldn't understand the point. "We weren't sure whether they thought we needed an extra start or they just said, 'Let's bring all the black kids together.'" The answer was, the university thought the students needed an extra start. The result was, by the time other students arrived, the students who had been there for Third World Orientation Week already had a circle of friends made up only of minorities.

As Michelle pointed out in her thesis, Princeton fell short of offering more meaningful solutions. It had only five tenured African American professors. The Afro-American Studies department offered only four courses in the spring semester of her senior year.

However, unlike the image of her presented by Barack's opponents, Michelle's reaction to the difficult environment of Princeton, which some of her classmates still describe with resentment, was noticeably calm. She didn't imagine insults, but she didn't ignore them when they happened.

Howard Taylor, former chair of the Center for African-American Studies and one of Michelle's thesis advisers, recalled Michelle's moderate position on the question of isolation and integration. "She was not an assimilationist, but she wasn't a wide-eyed militant either," Taylor said. "She was able to straddle that issue with great insight."

The lasting memory of her friends and professors is of a person who sounds much the same as she'd be described today: balanced, funny, energetic, devoted to her parents, and focused on things that matter. She was still academically ambitious, too. She didn't just plan to be a lawyer; she planned to go to one of the best law schools in the country, and the most prestigious, Harvard.

5

THE PAPER CHASE

One of the traditions at Harvard Law School is that parents buy space in the back of the yearbook to leave a message for their graduating children. In the 1988 edition, next to serious, almost formal messages of congratulations to Michelle's classmates, is a message from Michelle's parents to her: "We knew you would do this fifteen years ago when we could never make you shut up."

Just twenty-four years old, Michelle now had

two of the most respected academic degrees in the country. Doors would open for her. She'd be offered jobs starting at larger salaries than those her parents earned. If she did nothing more than avoid big mistakes, her career would continue to advance, thanks to the prestige of the Princeton and Harvard names. But as she had already found out, there was a price to pay for this kind of success. Not long after starting Harvard, she had called her former boss at the Third World Center, Czerny Brasuell, and admitted, "If I could do this over, I'm not sure I would."

She realized that she probably should have worked for a year after Princeton before deciding whether to go to law school. Instead, she had given in to common pressures. "The thing about these wonderful schools is they can be surprisingly narrowing to your perspective," she told reporter Rebecca Johnson. "You can be a lawyer or you can work on Wall Street; those are the conventional options. They're easy, socially acceptable, and financially rewarding. Why wouldn't you do it?" Earning money was important to Michelle. It was also urgent, because she had Princeton tuition loans to repay.

It's not that she hated law school. She just wasn't

thrilled by it. Unlike some of the students, she was happy to remain in the background of discussions. Professors who taught Barack a few years later remember him as much more involved in class debates. When Michelle did speak up, she was more likely to disagree with a teacher than with a fellow student. She wasn't interested in the competition that takes place between students at Harvard. But, true to her pattern, she challenged people in authority.

The most important part of her three years at Harvard was not in the classroom. She worked at a legal aid office that was run by the students. Poor clients who couldn't afford a lawyer to handle conflicts with a landlord or a divorce or a problem collecting money that was owed could go to the students for help. If the dispute had to go to court, an experienced lawyer might help, but otherwise the law students managed their own work. It was perfect for Michelle. She spent a lot of time at the legal aid center. Colleagues remember her as serious about her work, and good at it, but also fun to have in the office.

PURPLE POWER

Having gone to Harvard, it was hard to resist the obvious next step. She took a job at a large Chicago law firm, Sidley & Austin. At the time, her father, who had been working for the city for decades, was making $40,000. Her starting salary at age twenty-four was $65,000.

But despite her interest in and need for a good income, her desire for interesting work was hard to fulfill at Sidley.

Her bosses tried, even though some of them believed she was too demanding. Unfortunately, large firms use young lawyers for the less interesting parts of legal work. Sidley also didn't handle cases that were as satisfying to her as working for the legal aid clients had been.

Then one day a colleague came into her office with a videotape. The Corporation for Public Broadcasting had just bought a new television show, and they needed a Sidley lawyer to work on the copyright and merchandise rights. Michelle found a conference room with a videotape player and pushed the cassette into the slot. When she pushed the PLAY button,

TOP: On February 10, 2007, Barack began his candidacy for president in front of the Old State Capitol building in Springfield, Illinois. He chose the site where Abraham Lincoln delivered a famous speech calling for an end to the nation's angry political divisions. CENTER: Michelle begins the campaign in Iowa. BOTTOM: Facing reporters on the campaign plane.

© Emmanuel Dunand/AFP/Getty Images

© AP/Matt Rourke

© Jason Reed/Reuters/Corbis

© Rick Friedman/Corbis

© Linda Davidson/The Washington Post

© Doug Pensinger/Getty Images

© AP/Jack Dempsey

© AP/Jae C. Hong

OPPOSITE PAGE, CLOCKWISE FROM TOP LEFT: On the campaign trail: arriving at the Indianapolis airport; with pre-kindergarten students in Ardmore, Pennsylvania; in Manchester, New Hampshire; happy to be in Norfolk, Virginia; at a rally in Detroit. THIS PAGE, TOP: Michelle speaks at a volunteer day to aid troops during the 2008 Democratic National Convention in Denver. BOTTOM LEFT: Michelle listens to Staff Sgt. Ian Newland, an injured Iraq veteran at the event, while making care packages for troops overseas. BOTTOM RIGHT: In Indiana, Michelle hugs Abby Maddox, wife of a serviceman in Iraq.

Michelle set strict campaigning limits for herself to keep life as normal as possible for Malia and Sasha. She tried to campaign just two days a week and to fly back to Chicago before bedtime. TOP: With Sasha while Barack speaks in Iowa. LEFT: Michelle and Malia play at the Iowa State Fair. BOTTOM: During Barack's acceptance speech at the Democratic National Convention.

© Justin Sullivan/Getty Images

© Justin Sullivan/Getty Images

© AP/Paul Sancya

© Jim Bourg-Pool/Getty Images

© Ethan Miller/Getty Images

CLOCKWISE FROM TOP LEFT: Michelle's brother, Craig, and mother, Marian, meet President Jimmy Carter at the 2008 Democratic National Convention, where Barack would be named as the party's candidate. Barack and Michelle after the second presidential debate in Nashville, Tennessee. Michelle campaigning in Nevada. Michelle and Oprah Winfrey in New Hampshire.

LEFT: At the Iowa State Fair. MIDDLE: Cheers for Michelle at the convention. BOTTOM: Michelle's congratulatory dap (fist bump) earlier in the summer. "It captures what I love about my wife," Barack later said. "There's an irreverence about her and a sense that for all the hoopla, that I'm her husband and sometimes we'll do silly things."

© Scott Olson/Getty Images

© John Moore/Getty Images

© Scott Olson/Getty Images

TOP: In Chicago on Election Day, November 4, 2008. BELOW: After twenty-one months of campaigning, a historic victory that's watched by the world, and a new first lady.

© Stan Honda/AFP/Getty Images

Michelle Obama: An American story

a purple dinosaur danced across the screen and began to sing. Her new client was Barney. Work had just become a little more interesting.

Another of her assignments was to mentor a summer associate. Large law firms try to recruit top law school students to join their firms after graduation by bringing them to a grown-up version of summer camp. The summer associates are given a taste of legal work during the day, and in the evening—if they're interning at a competitive firm— they're treated to barbeques and baseball games and party cruises.

Some of Michelle's coworkers had met a particular summer associate during the interview process and somehow sensed that there'd be an attraction between him and Michelle. He was from Harvard Law, they said. He was older than the usual summer associates, because he hadn't gone to law school right after college. Sidley had taken him as a summer associate even though he had only finished his first year of law school. That was unusual. Apparently he was brilliant: His professors at Harvard were already talking about his future. The senior lawyers at Sidley were delighted that they'd snagged him. Just from the photo he'd sent in for the firm's directory there was a lot of giggling in the hallways about him being cute.

Michelle shook her head at all of it. "I had dated a lot of brothers who had this kind of reputation coming in," she told Obama biographer David Mendell. "I figured he was one of these smooth brothers who could talk straight and impress people." Michelle, who had always been about hard work, was skeptical that her colleagues even knew what to look for. "I figured that they were just impressed with any black man with a suit and a job," she later said.

They were impressed by more than that.

6

"HIS NAME IS BARACK"

Because she was going to be this new associate's mentor, Michelle looked for his picture in the directory Sidley was preparing. Not bad, she thought. But she quickly imagined a defect: His nose was too big.

That was typical of Michelle at the time. She had an instinct for self-defense. When she did date, she ended it before it could get serious. It was always the man's fault, she imagined. He fell short in some way.

Too much this, not enough that. Her brother began to pity them as soon as he met them. "There would be no reason for me to dislike any of my sister's boyfriends," he told the *Providence Journal*. "It was always more you sort of felt sorry for them because you knew it was just a matter of time before they were getting fired." Not much time, in fact. "She fired 'em fast," Craig said. There was always a reason, though it doesn't seem like the reason was always serious. "They'd do something and she'd say, 'That's it.'"

Michelle's explanation was that none of these boyfriends were as good as her father. She was waiting for someone who met the standard set by him. Her friends and family figured she'd be waiting a long time.

There was more to it, as there usually is. Sometimes her father's example was an excuse. When she was being tough on her boyfriends she was being tough on herself. She was trying to avoid making a mistake. Her perfectionist streak was coming out again. Like all perfectionists, a part of her worried that one wrong decision would mess up everything she'd accomplished. Anything that wasn't exactly right was totally wrong.

She also didn't want to get distracted by a boy-friend. As much as she wanted a family—and she wanted one a lot—she had worked hard to become a lawyer at Sidley, and there was more she wanted to do professionally.

All this gave her a hard shell. "My parents weren't very optimistic that I was going to find anybody who would put up with me," she told reporter Holly Yeager.

Then the summer associate who was supposedly a big deal arrived at the firm. Barack walked into her office and introduced himself.

Okay, she thought. *His nose isn't so big.* She was already starting to soften.

He was also tall, she noticed. She liked that. Michelle is 5'11" in bare feet, and she wears heels that make her taller. Barack is 6'2". *He's actually not bad looking*, she thought.

Barack's first impression of her: "Lovely." As he recalled it in his memoir *The Audacity of Hope*, Michelle had "a friendly, professional manner that matched her tailored suit and blouse."

Michelle was already playing it cool. She had her reasons, and at least one of them made sense: She was supposed to be his mentor at the firm. It wasn't the same as being his boss, but it was a professional relationship. She didn't think it was right to mix that with a personal relationship. Less reasonable: They were both African American. "I thought, 'Now how would that look?'" she told David Mendell. "Here we are, the only two black people here, and we are dating? I'm thinking that looks pretty tacky."

They actually weren't the only two African Americans at the firm, though there weren't many in their positions. She was right that people would have noticed. But why did she suddenly care so much about what other people thought about her personal life? What was behind that vague word, "tacky," that she used to dismiss the idea? That was not a word she'd have used to describe any other two African Americans who were dating. She wouldn't even have thought it if Barack had been dating someone else at the firm.

It may have been something more than her usual instinct to stay free from relationships. Professionally, she was still a rarity: a female African American graduate of Harvard Law. She knew from experience that to be effective she needed to keep clients and colleagues focused on the part of her that was a lawyer. This was something her white female colleagues also had to do. For Michelle it went double.

Barack didn't give up asking for a date. Michelle resisted, but not because she wasn't interested. She made a "proclamation" to her mother: "I'm not worrying about dating . . . I'm going to focus on me." Right.

She tried to deflect him by setting him up with her friends. He wasn't interested. She wasn't very disappointed.

Having fooled herself, Michelle thought she was doing a good job of hiding her feelings from everyone. But one of her colleagues, Mary Carragher, told biographer Liza Mundy that the courtship looked a little different from the outside. A few times Carragher would go to Michelle's office in the late afternoon and see Barack inside, sitting on the corner of Michelle's desk while he and Michelle were having a conversation that obviously wasn't about business. From the doorway, she could see that Michelle, usually so focused, had finally encountered a distraction she liked. *You know what*, Carragher would think before knocking, *I'm going back to my office*. After each of these conversations, Carragher told Mundy, Michelle would mention to Carragher something new she'd just learned about Barack. "She had all these little facts about him," Carragher said. She remembered Michelle's amazement when telling Carragher, "I can't believe he's got a *white grandmother from Kansas!*"

"She was falling hard," Carragher told Mundy, "But always cool." In his memoir *The Audacity of Hope*, Barack recalled that it was hard to melt the ice. He was only at Sidley for the summer, so he didn't think much of Michelle's excuse that she was his adviser. "Come on," he said to her. "What advice are you giving me? You're showing me how the copy machine works. You're telling me which restaurants to try. I don't think the partners will consider one date a serious breach of firm policy." When she kept refusing, he said, "OK, I'll quit [the firm]. How's that? You're my adviser. Tell me who I have to talk to."

The more interested Michelle became, the more careful she was. He was going back to Massachusetts at the end of the summer to finish law school, right? Then no, thank you. But she could resist only so much. "Eventually, I wore her down," Barack wrote. "After a firm picnic, she drove me back to my apartment and I offered to buy her an ice cream at the Baskin-Robbins store across the street." It turned into an unplanned date. "We sat on the curb and ate our ice creams in the sticky afternoon heat, and I told her about working at Baskin-Robbins when I was a teenager and how it was hard to look cool in a brown apron and cap. She told me that for a span of two or three years as a child, she had refused to eat anything except peanut butter and jelly. I asked if I could kiss her."

There were secret dates afterward—and at least one that wasn't secret. They bumped into a colleague at a movie theater. Michelle was embarrassed. But with friends outside of the law firm, she could finally open up. She called a friend from Harvard Law School, Verna Williams, to give her the news. "Guess what?" Michelle said. "I've got this great guy in my life. His name is Barack." She told Williams how it had happened, and she mentioned all the details about Barack that fascinated her. "It was clear she was pretty crazy about him." Williams remembered.

With her family, Michelle didn't gush about Barack. She didn't share with them the things she had learned about his family, and his childhood in Hawaii and Indonesia, and his reputation at Harvard Law School. Almost shyly, she brought him to her parents' house for a family dinner. She was also setting him up to be tested. She wasn't going to sell him to her family beforehand. He had to present himself. Of course, if they didn't like him, that would be the end.

But her family had been through this before, so they had sympathy for Barack. "First impression was that he was smart, easygoing, good sense of humor," Craig remembered. "I thought, 'Too bad he won't be around for long.'" As he recalls, his parents felt the same way. "We gave it a month, tops. Not because there was anything wrong with him . . . but we knew he was going to do something wrong, and then it was going to be too bad for him."

They weren't worried that Michelle might lose something special. Barack's unusual background and his education might have interested them, but Barack didn't talk about himself. They had no idea he had a white mother, and they wouldn't know for a long time. It wasn't a secret. He just never mentioned it. They didn't hear that he planned to run for a prestigious position at Harvard Law School, editor of the *Harvard Law Review*, which surely would have interested all of them. So Michelle's family, who assumed they'd never see him again, didn't take any special interest in him. Final verdict after the dinner? "He was just another one who wasn't going to make it."

Then, about a month after the dinner, Craig got a call from Michelle. She wanted a favor. It was about Barack. Craig was surprised Barack was still around. But what did she want?

"My father and I had a theory that you can really tell what somebody's personality is like by playing basketball with him," Craig remembered. Is he generous with his passes? Does he take the shot when it's his? Is he a show-off? Does he lie about fouling or being fouled? Can you trust him to keep score? Michelle wanted Craig to invite Barack to play basketball and then give her his opinion of Barack's character.

Craig's first thought was, "Oh, no, she's going to

make me be the bad guy." But he went along with it. He invited Barack to an informal game.

Barack got some credit just for showing up. After starring for Princeton, Craig had been drafted in the fourth round by the Philadelphia 76ers and then had played professionally in Europe. Pickup games with Craig were serious. Craig was also 6'6" to Barack's 6'2", and Craig ran with other big players. Many years later, in 2001, when Michael Jordan was preparing for a possible comeback with the Washington Wizards, Craig was one of the players chosen for secret practice games to tune up the superstar. Craig was almost forty years old then. When he played Barack, he was closer to twenty-seven. Barack hadn't played organized basketball since high school. He was pretty good then—though maybe not as good as he imagined at the time.

They met at a school. Barack and Craig were on the same team. Craig saw that Barack was left-handed, and knew how to pick spots on the court where that was an advantage. *Okay*, Craig thought. *Smart*. Barack couldn't easily drive to basket against Craig's bigger friends, but he had an outside shot. *That took some practice.* Just as Michelle had hoped,

Craig got a sense of Barack's character. "I was happy to report back he was a good guy on the court," Robinson told the *Providence Journal* many years later, when millions more people were wondering what personality traits Barack had revealed that day. "He was confident without being cocky. He was intense. He wanted to win. If he thought a call needed to be argued, he'd argue, but mostly he just played with a lot of integrity. And he didn't just pass the ball to me because I was Michelle's brother."

Craig came away from the game a lot more interested in Barack, who in his own quiet way showed a stronger character than Craig had expected. His parents soon felt the same way. "My sister is one tough girl," Craig remembered. "I'm older and I'm still afraid of her. She's very accomplished, so she needs someone as accomplished as her, and she also needs someone who can stand up to her. So, we in the family, we were just hoping that she could hang on to this guy, because it was readily apparent he could stand up to her."

"THEN AND THERE, I DECIDED"

Barack knew how to get through to Michelle. Some of their dates were unconventional, like when he took her to church basements for community meetings he had organized. But he was able to show off a side of himself that he knew she'd admire. "He connected with me and everyone in that church basement," she remembered. "He was able to articulate a vision that resonated with people, that was real. And right then and there, I decided this guy was special. The authenticity you see is real, and that's why I fell in love with him." Although she was focused on earning a living, she admired Barack's lack of interest in money. "He could've gone to Wall Street. Those offers were available to him. But instead Barack bussed these young mothers down to City Hall to help them find their voice and advocate for change." She also loved his ability to stay hopeful that his work was worth it. "He talked about the simple notion that we as Americans understand the world as it is—and it is a world sometimes that is disappointing and unfair—but our job as American citizens is to work toward building the world as it should be."

Barack also understood a different side of her than anyone else did—even her family. He wrote in *The Audacity of Hope*, "There was a glimmer that danced across her round, dark eyes whenever I looked at her, the slightest hint of uncertainty, as if, deep inside, she knew how fragile things really were, and that if she ever let go, even for a moment, all her plans might quickly unravel."

She needed someone who saw past the tough exterior to that part of her. Barack was the first. Much later, Craig, who might have known her better than anyone, said he was surprised by that insight.

But at the end of the summer, Barack had to return to Cambridge, Massachusetts, for his second year of Harvard Law School. Could the relationship survive the distance? There would be another year after that before he was finished. For him, a long-distance relationship would be something new.

He knew Michelle was worth it, and the relationship lasted. But these two strong personalities had different ideas about where it was leading. Michelle recalled to *New Yorker* reporter Lauren Collins, "We would have this running debate throughout our relationship about whether marriage was necessary. It was sort of a bone of contention, because I was, like, 'Look, buddy, I'm not one of these who'll just hang out forever.' You know, that's just not who I am." But Barack wasn't easily pushed, Michelle remembered. He'd say, "'Marriage, it doesn't mean anything, it's really how you feel.' And I was, like, 'Yeah, right.'"

They dated for three years. Michelle had just about had enough when Barack took her out to a dinner at a luxurious restaurant in Chicago. It was supposed to be a celebration of his passing the bar exam, so he could practice law in Illinois. Naturally, the question came up: Law school's done, so now what? He was a little vague, and toward the end of the meal he began to repeat all the same old arguments against marriage. "He got me into one of these discussions again," she remembered. She was "fired up," and he was "blah blah blah blah" with his ideas that a piece of paper didn't make a difference.

That was it. She'd waited long enough for him to come around. But just as she was about to tell him, she was interrupted by the waiter: "Dessert comes out, the tray comes out, and there's a ring!"

The were married in October 1992. The wedding was almost as Michelle had always imagined it, and it was almost a perfect day. Almost. Someone she'd always thought would be there, maybe the person she counted on the most, wasn't there. As happy as she was on her wedding day, a loss had already begun to change her life in ways would that shock some of the people who knew her best.

7

WHERE THE HEART IS

In 1991, about a year and a half before Michelle
and Barack were married, Michelle's father died.
He was just fifty-five years old. He'd had surgery
for a kidney operation, and there were complications.

Michelle was shattered. Although she had worried
about his health for as long as she could remember,
she wasn't prepared for his sudden death at such a
young age.

In his memoir *The Audacity of Hope*, Barack recalled

flying back to Chicago for the funeral and holding Michelle as the casket was lowered. Right then, he made a silent promise to Fraser to take care of Michelle.

She would need his help. She had already been shaken the year before by the death of one of her closest friends, who had died of cancer at just twenty-five.

CONSUMING PASSIONS

Suzanne Alele had been a classmate at Princeton, where she'd arrived after a childhood as varied as Barack's: Born in Nigeria, raised in Jamaica and then Washington, D.C., she was both an athelete and a computer geek. She was less serious than Michelle, and she often told Michelle to relax about the future and enjoy herself more. Although her example hadn't been enough to draw Michelle off the academic path, Michelle was tempted.

Michelle was at Alele's bedside when her friend passed away. The experience caused Michelle to think about her friend's attitude toward life, and how it differed from her own. She asked herself, "If I died in four months, is this how I would have wanted to spend this time? I started thinking about the fact that I went to some of the best schools in the country and I have no idea what I want[ed] to do." She suddenly understood that her pursuit of excellence at Princeton and Harvard had narrowed her life, not widened it. She explained to reporter Richard Wolffe, "You can make money and have a nice degree. But what are you learning about giving back to the world, and finding your passion and letting that guide you, as opposed to the school you got into?"

She was about to walk away from certain success. A senior lawyer at her law firm later said that if she had stayed with the firm "she would have been a superstar." But, Michelle recalled, "I looked out at my neighborhood and sort of had an epiphany that I had to bring my skills to bear in the place that made me," she later told the *New York Times*. "I wanted to have a career motivated by passion and not just money."

The problem was, money makes a difference when you owe a lot of it, and Michelle did. The student loans from Princeton and Harvard weighed heavily on her. But worrying too much about money also felt wrong to her. As she put it years later, she didn't want to roll up to the family reunion in a Mercedes-Benz.

Barack's influence tipped the balance. He has never been as practical as Michelle, so it was easy for him to tell her to follow her heart. Money? He didn't notice it when he had it. His car at the time had a rust hole on the passenger side that was so big Michelle could see the street go by. Later, when he was a state senator, he would put government expenses on personal credit cards and forget to ask for repayment.

Michelle's family, however, wasn't so casual. Her father was still alive at the time, and he asked, "Don't you want to pay your student loans?" Her college roommate Angela Acree could barely believe what Michelle was planning to do. "I'm sure at Sidley she made more money than her parents ever made," Acree recalled. "It just seemed incredible at the time that she'd leave."

But along with pushing Michelle toward academic success, her parents had taught her to do what would make her happy. She was following that advice.

She was also following the example of people who'd helped create opportunities for her, like the activists who had pushed Chicago in the 1960s from the era of "Willis Wagon" portable classrooms to high schools like Whitney M. Young. She told Mary Mitchell of the *Chicago Sun-Times*, "I did exactly what leaders in my community told me to do. They said do your best in school, work hard, study, get into the best schools you can get into and when you do that, baby, you bring that education back and you work in your communities."

Michelle wrote to several charities and government agencies. One letter was passed along to Valerie Jarrett, deputy chief of staff to Chicago mayor Richard M. Daley.

The mayor was the son of the Richard J. Daley, who had run the city's Democratic political machine during Michelle's childhood. Michelle didn't have good memories of that. Her father's experiences as a precinct captain had made the whole family suspicious of politicians. The first Daley had fought to keep African Americans in small neighborhoods and poor schools.

But Michelle went to an interview with Jarrett anyway. They liked each other instantly. Instead of lasting for a polite fifteen minutes, the interview went on for an hour and a half. They learned about each other. Jarrett's background and experience were fascinating. She was born in Iran, where her American father, a doctor, was running a children's hospital. As a child she lived in London before the family moved back to Chicago. Her father, grandfather, and great-grandfather all broke barriers for African Americans. Jarrett had become a lawyer and then ahd devoted herself to public service. Michelle could see that Jarrett didn't believe in old-style Chicago politics.

Jarrett could also see that Michelle would be a huge help to the city. "I offered her a job at the end of the interview," Jarrett remembered, "which was totally inappropriate since it was the mayor's decision. She was so confident and committed and extremely open."

Michelle didn't accept right away. Because Barack shared her doubts about city hall, she asked Jarrett to meet with Barack. Jarrett convinced him. In fact, she later became one of his closest advisers.

Michelle was put in charge of simplifying and solving any problems that businesses and citizens were having with city hall. There was a lot less money than she'd been earning at Sidley, but there was more satisfaction. She then became assistant commissioner of planning and development. That job let her focus on solving the problems with Chicago neighborhoods that had led to conflict in the city when she was growing up.

"SHE BUILT IT TO LAST"

About a year and a half after joining the mayor's office, Michelle got another opportunity. A charity called Public Allies, which had been founded the year before in Washington, D.C., had chosen Chicago as the location of its second office. (It now has almost twenty.) With a combination of volunteer work and education, Public Allies develops young people who want to become community service leaders. The Washington staff had heard of Barack's reputation as a community organizer and wanted him to run the Chicago office. He told them the person they really needed was Michelle. They were soon happy he did.

Paul Schmitz, chief executive officer of Public Allies, remembered, "At a time when the average age of our staff was twenty-three, she was like drafting Brett Favre for the Packers," Schmitz told Jay Newton-Small of TIME. "Michelle was twenty-nine when we hired her. She had a law degree from Harvard, had worked for the mayor, for a corporate law firm. Comparatively, I'd worked a telemarketing group. Frankly, we were surprised that she wanted to do it."

Michelle recalled that it was a leap of faith. "It sounded risky and just out there," she told Richard Wolffe. "But for some reason it just spoke to me. This was the first time I said, 'This is what I say I care about. Right here. And I will have to run it.'" She got a new title, executive director, and another pay cut.

It didn't take long for Michelle to stamp the office with her personal style. Vanessa Kirsch, a founder of Public Allies, remembered, "She had incredibly high expectations and was constantly asking questions, making sure we were using her time well. There were days when, even though she worked for me, I definitely felt like I worked for her."

Nothing was done halfway. Barbara Pace-Moody, another community leader in Chicago, told reporter Lauren Collins she recalled meeting Michelle around this time when they were both volunteering for a program to mentor young women, before Michelle and Barack were married: "We had a big gala, and she and her sister-in-law took their own money and paid for the girls to get their hair done and set them up in a hotel downtown. I remember thinking, Who is this Michelle Robinson?"

Michelle was tough enough to work in Cabrini-Green, a notorious housing project that some Chicago police officers refused to enter. She became the authority the young volunteers needed: "She let nothing slide," remembered José A. Rico, an illegal immigrant who had a fantasy about opening a high school for Latinos. Thanks in part to her help, he became a citizen, helped start a high school, and became its principal. She also helped many of the young people through their first close relationships with people of different backgrounds. Being the boss, she was able to do that in her own way, which didn't emphasize being nice or politically correct. "Real change," she explained to the *New York Times*, "comes from having enough comfort to be really honest and say something very uncomfortable."

Michelle stayed at Public Allies for four years. The Chicago office became the strongest in the country.

Michelle had built a board of advisers who could carry it into the future and raised funds so successfully that she left behind enough money to run the office for a year. A dozen years later, no other director has matched that. As Public Allies's Paul Schmitz said, "She built it to last."

Her own future, however, had become much less certain. While she was at Public Allies, Barack was frustrated by his own career. Although he was at a law firm that handled a lot of community service work, his cases hadn't led to the sweeping changes he hoped to achieve. He had decided it wasn't enough to ask judges to interpret the law his way. He wanted to write the laws in the first place. That meant he had to run for political office.

8

BRINGING UP BARACK

Barack wanted to begin his political career by running for the Illinois State Senate. It was 1995, and he was about to turn thirty-four. Michelle was thirty-one and eager to have children. Barack's decision scared her. She knew it would take a lot of his time. Also, the capital of Illinois is Springfield, which can be a three-hour trip from Chicago. She'd be left home alone when he had stretches of business in the capital. Going into politics would also mean Barack would give up the possibility of a good salary at his law firm. By now, Michelle was used to Barack's lack of interest in money, but she still knew they would need it to raise children comfortably.

In the end, however, she supported him. She wasn't sure if he was doing the right thing, but she knew from how hard he worked to convince her that it was the thing he wanted.

Barack ran in a district that was safe for a Democrat. The person who was giving up the position, Alice Palmer, was leaving only because she wanted to run for the U.S. Congress. After winning the election in November 1996, Barack was sworn in with the rest of the Senate in January 1997.

His political career had begun. With it, problems had also begun for Michelle and for their marriage.

INVISIBLE MAN

hen Barack was in the Illinois State Senate, the Democratic Party was in the minority. Barack did not have the influence on public policy that he had hoped to have.

Being a first-year senator, he had little influence even within the Democratic Party. It was frustrating.

Michelle had just started a new job herself, at the University of Chicago. Her presence there was a sign of how far the city had come. When she was growing up, the university, despite being just a few blocks from her home, was a separate world. It didn't seem to notice the community around it. "I grew up five minutes from the university and never once went on campus," she recalled to reporter Holly Yeager. "All the buildings have their backs to the community. The university didn't think kids like me existed, and I certainly didn't want anything to do with that place." But the university wanted to change. By this time, Michelle's work for Public Allies had made her known throughout the city. The university wanted her, badly. It created a new position for her: associate dean of student services and director of the university community service center. Her job was to encourage students to volunteer in the community, and to show them how to do it. Once again, she was inside an institution that had contributed to conflict in Chicago when she was growing up, and she was helping to change it.

As always, Michelle was determined to do a good job. Although she supported Barack's political ambitions, she could not give him all her time or attention. If anything, Michelle had to demand more of these things from him.

In July 1998, their daughter Malia Ann was born. Now Michelle was a working mother with an infant child and a husband whose job was three hours away. Even when he was in Chicago, there were a lot of demands on his time. Politicians have to go to a lot of parties, whether or not they want to. On top of all that, Barack was teaching law at the University of Chicago.

Barack's solution to his own frustration wasn't to drop out of politics, but instead to aim higher. He decided to run for the U.S. Congress in the 2000 election.

Michelle was much less supportive of this desire. In his memoir *The Audacity of Hope*, he recalled that "My wife's anger toward me seemed barely contained. 'You only think about yourself,' she would tell me. 'I never thought I'd have to raise a family alone.'"

He lost that election. But he was still in the state senate, so the pressures remained. Then Natasha

(Sasha) was born in June 2001. Michelle was so angry at Barack's absences that she could barely stand to speak to him on one family vacation in Hawaii. Making it worse, the governor needed Barack to return to Springfield early to vote on an important bill. Barack made the decision to stay in Hawaii, and the bill failed to pass, which caused him difficulty with the governor and led to criticism from journalists. But that was easier to face than more of Michelle's anger.

Michelle's solution was to demand less, but also to train Barack. She wouldn't ask him to be around more. But when he was around, she'd make sure he helped more. She started going to the gym long before dawn. When the girls woke up and needed to be fed, he'd have to feed them. "I spent a lot of time expecting my husband to fix things," she told Rebecca Johnson of *Vogue*. "But then I came to realize that he was there in the ways he could be. If he wasn't there, it didn't mean he wasn't a good father or didn't care. I saw it could be my mom or a great baby-sitter who helped. Once I was okay with that, my marriage got better."

Michelle also kept working. The University of Chicago Medical Center hired her to improve its poor relations with the community. She helped erase decades of mistrust with straight talk about the longstanding problems.

Around the same time, she helped her brother make the same decision she'd made earlier. After Princeton, Craig earned an MBA and went to Wall Street. He stayed there nine years, became a vice president and a millionaire, and then joined a Chicago financial firm where his success continued. But he was miserable. He didn't like the work. His unhappiness was one of the reasons he was in the middle of a divorce. What he really wanted to do, he told Michelle, was coach basketball. He had a chance to do that, at a low level and for a tiny fraction of what he had been earning. Should he? Michelle told him to do what she'd done: Follow his heart. Now he's one of the happiest head coaches in basketball. "I'm loving every day of my life," he says.

Unfortunately, Barack and Michelle's money problems didn't go away. When Barack traveled to Los

Angeles for the Democratic National Convention in 2000, he discovered at the airport's car rental counter that he couldn't rent a car because he'd reached the limit on his credit card.

Every day Michelle took a more practical view of their lives. Part of her hoped that Barack would come around to her way of thinking, and walk away from the world of politics. But although she was still the planner and the worrier in the family, Barack was still the dreamer. In late 2001, he began to think about a run for the U.S. Senate in 2004.

Michelle thought he was crazy—and that was before she heard how he planned to make it happen.

SHEER AUDACITY

Michelle later told biographer David Mendell, "The big issue around the Senate for me was, how on earth can we afford it? I don't like to talk about it, because people forget that his credit card was maxed out. How are we going to get by? Okay, now we're going to have two households to fund, one here and one in Washington.

We have law school debt, tuition to pay for the children. And we're trying to save for college for the girls. . . . My thing is, is this just another gamble? It's just killing us. My thing was, this is ridiculous, even if you do win, how are you going to afford this wonderful next step in your life? And he said, 'Well, then, I'm going to write a book, a good book.' And I'm thinking, '. . . Just write a book, yeah, that's right. Yep, yep, yep. And you'll climb the beanstalk and come back down with the golden egg, Jack.'"

Barack worked hard to convince her. He told her he really wanted to make a difference, and this seemed like the best way. He told her he'd give up politics if he lost this time. She gave in. "Whatever," she told him. "We'll figure it out. We're not hurting. Go ahead." Then, as she told David Mendell, she added a hopeful thought: "Maybe you'll lose."

Barack would write the book a few years later. It would be his second memoir, *The Audacity of Hope*. But he took a practical approach to the first problem of the campaign: finding someone to run it. After a lot of trying, he won the help of an experienced political adviser, David Axelrod. Axelrod came up with a slogan: "Yes, we can"—the same message that, without the comma, they would use for the 2008 presidential campaign.

Barack still wasn't widely known, but he and Axelrod and their team worked steadily to change that. They also believed that their opponents, whom they knew well, would stumble. That's exactly what happened. It looked as though Barack could keep gaining right up to Election Day. Then an opportunity came for Barack to deliver a knockout punch: He was asked to give the opening speech at the 2004 Democratic National Convention, a few months before the election.

Barack had been hoping for more Illinois media, and now the national media swarmed him. His team sweated every detail of the speech for weeks. Everyone became tense as the big night in Boston approached. There was even a last-minute debate about his tie in his hotel room. A switch was made for a tie that an aide happened to be wearing.

Michelle noticed that the nervousness of everyone around him was starting to wear on Barack. Just before he went on stage for this speech that would either launch or end his national career, she made him relax with her wicked sense of humor. That's when she told him, "Just don't screw it up, buddy."

He didn't. "There's not a liberal America and a conservative America—there's a *United States of America*," he declared. "There's not a black America and a white America and a Latino America and an Asian America—there's the *United States of America*. . . . We are one people. . . ."

Four months later, he was a U.S. senator.

He was sworn in the following January. After the ceremony, the Obamas stepped outside the Capitol, followed by reporters and photographers. Malia, who was six, looked up at Barack proudly and asked, "Daddy, are you going to be president?"

The press laughed at Barack's embarrassment. But when Barack didn't answer, a reporter for the *Chicago Tribune* asked, "Well, Senator . . . ?"

9

THE SPOTLIGHT

That day in Washington, Barack didn't answer the reporters—or Malia. He knew better than to admit his ambition. There was a time when he wasn't so guarded.

Back when Michelle and Barack were first dating, about fourteen or fifteen years earlier, Barack had won a position approximately as prestigious as his new Senate seat, and just as difficult to achieve: Michelle's steady boyfriend. He had made it as far as coming to a Robinson holiday party to meet the Michelle's extended family. The first person he caught up with was Craig. They hadn't seen much of each other since the basketball game, when Craig tested Barack as a favor to Michelle. Still playing the role of Michelle's big brother, Craig gave Barack a friendly quiz. What was Barack planning to do after Harvard Law? Meaning, How serious are you about my sister, and are you going to start a family or what?

"I'd like to teach." Barack said. "And maybe someday run for office."

"Oh, like city council?" Craig asked.

"No," Barack said. "Maybe the Senate. Possibly even president."

"President? President of *what*?"

"President of the United States maybe."

"Okaaay," Craig said, as if Barack had just mentioned spending a week on Mars. "Why don't you come over here and meet my Aunt Gracie? But don't tell anybody that!"

ONE WOMAN, ONE VOTE

Barack wanted it. People were telling him to do it. That's a powerful combination. The only thing that could have kept him from running, maybe, was Michelle. He needed her vote before he could ask for any others.

Michelle had questions. A lot of questions. She and the top staff he'd assembled for the Senate run had two long meetings to discuss them. She hadn't been closely involved in his campaigns up to that time, so for some of them it was a first experience with Michelle's focus on planning ahead and preparing for the worst. "I took myself down every dark road you could go on, just to prepare myself before we jumped out there," she told Gwen Ifill. "Are we emotionally, financially ready for this? I dreamed out all the scenarios." She did not want this to be an "ego trip" for Barack. She needed to know it was serious. Could they win? How? What would that mean for her and Malia and Sasha?

Some of her questions were practical: Where would the money come from? Hillary Clinton already seemed to have the support of all the usual donors.

Could they build a national team to rival Clinton's? There wasn't much time to do that, and many of the nation's best professional campaign staffers were already committed to Clinton. Could Barack win in the primary contests, which select the Democratic nominee, without the votes of women? They had been key to his success in the past, but, again, Clinton would be likely to win their support. Besides Clinton, who else might Barack have to face? If Barack ran and lost, how much debt would he and Michelle have? How could it be paid? She also asked about security. She knew that because of his racial background Barack would face more threats than the usual candidate.

She had philosophical questions, too. Would Barack have to compromise his beliefs to win votes nationally? Would he have to take a vague position on complicated issues so that he didn't offend anyone?

Barack's team gave her thoughtful answers. She gave Barack her okay. As she told reporter Melinda Henneberger, "Eventually I thought, This is a smart man with a good heart, and if the only reason I wouldn't want him to be president is that I'm married to him, no, I can't be that selfish."

ON THE ROAD

Michelle trusted Barack's team to do what they'd said, and she focused her attention on keeping life as normal as possible for Malia and Sasha. Her ideal family life remained the same as it was when she was growing up: everyone at home for family dinners and conversation. But after Barack's formal announcement of his candidacy in February 2007, the campaign needed her. Voters like to meet the wives of candidates. Michelle was also better than anyone at telling voters why they should vote for Barack—some days, she was better at that than Barack was.

To make it work, she had strict rules for the campaign. They could arrange appearances only on certain days. Michelle couldn't travel on days with important events like soccer games and ballet recitals. Most difficult of all, she had to fly back home before her daughters' bedtime. "Yeah, I'm a little tired at the end of the day," she told Gwen Ifill. "But the girls, they just think Mommy was at work. They don't know I was in New Hampshire. Quite frankly, they don't care." When she had to stay away overnight, her mother took care of Malia and Sasha. What did the girls really care about? The puppy they had been promised when the campaign was over.

As the campaign went on, her mother retired to help Michelle all the time, and she's now part of their lives in the White House. "Thank God for Grandma!" Michelle said to audiences during the campaign. It wasn't what Marian Robinson expected, but she said it wasn't hard. "Michelle is such a disciplinarian," she told reporter Rebecca Johnson, "there really isn't much for me to do." Michelle disagrees. Referring both to her own childhood and the help she gets now, Michelle told Melinda Henneberger, "Mama always understates her role."

To keep the girls in touch with Barack, Michelle bought two Apple Macbooks so they could have video chats. "It's harder for him, being on the road," Michelle told Holly Yeager during the campaign. "I've got my girls and our routine. I am feeling their love. He is missing that."

COMIC RELIEF

It took a while for the country to figure out Michelle. Her sense of humor was surprising. A political wife who made fun of her husband? Even the people who knew her well wondered if the voters would understand. "Occasionally, it gives campaign people heartburn," David Axelrod, the campaign's chief strategist told Lauren Collins of the *New Yorker*. "She's fundamentally honest—goes out there, speaks her mind, jokes. She doesn't parse her words or select them with an antenna for political correctness." When Collins asked Michelle if she was offended when Bill Clinton called Barack's opposition to the Iraq War a "fairy tale," Michelle gave the political answer: a simple "No." Then she made a horror-movie voice and held her hands up as if her fingernails were claws. "I want to rip his eyes out!" A nervous look from someone on her staff led her to state the obvious to the reporter: "Kidding!" she said. "See, this is what gets me into trouble."

At times it was difficult for her to keep smiling. Along with attacks from her opponents, and from some of the media, there was a constant stream of extreme, personal anger that flowed from the Internet. "You are amazed sometimes at how deep the lies can be," she told the *New York Times*. A lot of the hatred was connected to race. People who seemed to be angry at the idea of African Americans in the White House tried to spread the idea that Michelle hated white people. At one point, there was a rumor on the Internet that an audio recording of her calling Caucasians "whitey" was about to surface. "I mean, 'whitey'?" she said. "That's something that [1970s sitcom character] George Jefferson would say. Anyone who says that doesn't know me. They don't know the life I've lived. They don't know anything about me." There was no recording.

Hillary Clinton's criticism of Barack also stung. Michelle seemed to share a common opinion that Clinton was making race an issue. When ABC News asked Michelle if she would be able to support Clinton if Clinton were the party's nominee, Michelle said, "I'd have to think about that. I'd have to think about [her] policies, her approach, her tone." She was criticized for showing anger. She told reporter Richard Wolffe at the time, "It's like I can't think out loud."

The media's attacks became ugly. A caption on Fox News called her "Obama's baby mama," an insulting term for an unwed mother that included a wink toward her race. Fox later called the fist pound that she gave Barack at the Democratic National Convention a "terrorist fist jab."

She didn't help herself when she said in February 2008, as Barack was clinching the nomination, "for the first time in my adult life, I am really proud of my country." Had she said she was more proud than she'd ever been before, no one could have argued. But in the part of the political world that saw any Democrat as anti-American, and any African American as hostile to whites, her comment was repeated endlessly.

At the time, her brother Craig explained it to reporter Mark Patinkin as if it were a basketball game. Barack was beating the Clinton team, and later he was beating Senator John McCain's team. "When a team is down, they try everything they can to come back," Craig said. "Elbows, fouling you. And this is so much bigger. So the tactics are going to be what they're going to be."

A couple of things helped ease the sting of the insults. The first was that the attacks seemed to backfire on Barack's opponents. First Clinton, then McCain and then his running mate, vice-presidential candidate Sarah Palin, seemed to lose support each time they attacked the characters of Barack and Michelle. At the same time, Michelle's star rose. The more the voters saw of her, the more they liked her. That's part of why the attacks backfired. Craig said the difference was "magical." He told reporter Kristen Gelineau, "It's like going to sleep and waking up and you're Tinkerbell."

With weeks left to go before Election Day, November 4, 2008, Michelle and Barack knew they were almost certain to win. The polls from both the Democratic and Republican sides were consistent. Only a sudden news event could have affected the result. John McCain knew that, too.

The Obama campaign was determined to race to the finish line as hard as possible, but the worst part of the worrying was over. Now Michelle had to think about what would come next. As always, she was considering every possibility. But she didn't waste time wondering about which first lady she would use as a role model. "I don't think I can honestly emulate somebody else," she told Richard Wolffe. "I think I can only be who I can be in this role. And that's going to come with all the pluses and minuses and baggage and insecurities and all the things that I'll bring into it, plus my hopes and dreams along with it."

Some of those dreams are personal. For the self-described "Mom-in-Chief," one benefit of moving into the White House is that Barack will be working from home. After all of Barack's time as a state senator in Springfield, Illinois, then as a U.S. Senator in Washington, D.C., and finally as a presidential candidate for twenty months, Michelle finally has her whole family under one roof.

There are also grander hopes. At the Democratic National Convention a few months earlier, she had expressed the one constant theme in her life: "Barack and I . . . want our children—and all children in this nation—to know that the only limit to the height of your achievements is the reach of your dreams and your willingness to work hard for them."

Her example is already proof of that. ✦

ACKNOWLEDGMENTS

Laurie Brown is the reason there's a book.

Thanks to Laurie also for putting it in the hands of Jen Haller, Julia Richardson, Sheila Smallwood, Helena Chandler, Donna McCarthy, Margaret Melvin, John Mendelson, and Betsy Groban.

Thank you to Mark McVeigh, Nancy and Stanley Colbert, Magdalena Alagna, Jill Holt, Mark Grishaber, and Sonia Matthews, for everything.

Many thanks to William Rinehart, Pete and Gethyn

Soderman, Randy and Vicki Sturgill, and to the many volunteers and staff in Wilmington, North Carolina, including Chris Bramley, Heather Matheson, Sarah Reamer, Justin Schardin, and Nathan Williams.

NOTES

INTRODUCTION

"Can Michelle Obama Be First Lady No Matter What?":
Wonkette, November 13, 2007 (wonkette.com/322259/
can-michelle-obama-be-first-lady-no-matter-what).

"There is no difference": Richard Wolffe, "Barack's Rock,"
Newsweek, February 25, 2008.

"Nothing is fake": Kim Chipman, "Coach Robinson Knows
Real Michelle Obama Amid Attacks," *Bloomberg*, July 22,
2008.

"My daughters are doing chores": "Barack Obama: The
Barbara Walters Interview," ABC News, November 26,
2008.

"Just don't screw it up, buddy": Barack Obama, *The Audacity of Hope* (New York: Crown/Random House, 2006), 359.

CHAPTER 1

"pass a test just by carrying a book under his arm," "as good or better": Wolffe; "Barack's Rock."

"my mentor, my protector, and my lifelong friend": Michelle Obama, Remarks at the Democratic National Convention, August 25, 2008. Transcript from the *New York Times*, August 26, 2008.

"She might seem intimidating at first because she's so smart": Rebecca Johnson, "Michelle Obama's the Natural," *Vogue*, September 2007.

"Some of my earliest memories": Michelle Obama, "Democratic Radio Address," October 25, 2008.

"because [politics] seems like a dirty business": Melinda Henneberger, "Michelle Obama Interview: Her Father's Daughter," *Reader's Digest*, October 2008.

"reluctant participant": Holly Yeager, "The Heart and Mind of Michelle Obama," *O Magazine*, November 2007.

"I generally have shielded her from most of my campaigns": Yeager, "The Heart and Mind of Michelle Obama."

"we as a family were extremely cynical": Liza Mundy, "A Series of Fortunate Events," *Washington Post*, August 12, 2007. See also: Liza Mundy, *Michelle* (New York: Simon and Schuster, 2008), 27.

"People ask me about my kids now": Johnson, "Michelle Obama's the Natural."

"My dad was our rock," "He was our champion, our hero": Michelle Obama, Remarks at the Democratic National Convention, August 25, 2008.

"always had a smile on his face": Mundy, *Michelle*, 42.

"Seeing a parent with a disability": Henneberger, "Michelle Obama Interview: Her Father's Daughter."

"As he got sicker": Michelle Obama, Remarks at the Democratic National Convention, August 25, 2008.

"He didn't complain": Mary Mitchell, "Makeup's Too Much Work for Michelle," *Chicago Sun-Times*, August 7, 2007.

"one of those people . . . who are always preparing": Henneberger, "Michelle Obama Interview: Her Father's Daughter."

"When you have a parent with a disability": Yeager, "The Heart and Mind of Michelle Obama."

"She never takes a pass": Johnson, "Michelle Obama's the Natural."

"You never wanted to disappoint him": Wolffe, "Barack's Rock."

"If he was disappointed in you": Yeager, "The Heart and Mind of Michelle Obama."

"We always felt": David Mendell, *Obama: From Promise to Power* (New York: HarperCollins, 2007), 95.

"I always say Michelle raised herself": Cassandra West, "Her Plan Went Awry, but Michelle Obama Doesn't Mind," *Chicago Tribune*, September 1, 2004.

"It was the greatest gift a child could receive": Michelle Obama, Remarks at the Democratic National Convention, August 25, 2008.

"the smallest room I had ever seen": Rosalind Rossi, "Obama's Anchor," *Chicago Sun-Times*, January 21, 2007.

"somehow . . . she has managed to commit to memory": Craig Robinson, Remarks at the Democratic National Convention, August 25, 2008.

"We told them, 'Make sure you respect your teachers,'": Lauren Collins, "The Other Obama: Michelle Obama and the Politics of Candor," *The New Yorker*, March 10, 2008.

"I always resented it": Harriette Cole, "From a Mother's Eyes," *Ebony*, September, 2008.

"Yeah, she's got a temper": Susan Saulny, "Michelle Obama Thrives in Campaign Trenches," *New York Times*, February 14, 2008.

"Life's not fair": M. Charles Bakst, "Brown Coach Robinson a Strong Voice for Brother-in-law Obama," *Providence Journal*, May 20, 2007.

"When we were young kids, our parents divided the bedroom": Craig Robinson, Remarks at the Democratic National Convention, August 25, 2008.

"If you aren't challenged": Yeager, "The Heart and Mind of Michelle Obama."

"If I can't do it fast": Yeager, "The Heart and Mind of Michelle Obama."

"The academic part": Desmond Vonner, "Coach Has His Own Campaign," *Hartford Courant*, February 28, 2008.

CHAPTER 2

"It was back-breaking work": Leigh Pressley, "Building a Rice Empire Was Difficult Work," *Charlotte Observer*, July 9, 2008.

"In the summers": Dusinberre, William, *Them Dark Days: Slavery in the American Rice Swamps* (New York: Oxford University Press, 1995), 312.

"No region offered such fabulous fortunes": William Freehling, *The Road to Disunion* (New York: Oxford University Press, 1991), 214.

"I am actually so startled": Freehling, *Road to Disunion*, 215.

"a seedbed of black culture": Charles Joyner, *Shared Traditions: Southern History and Southern Culture* (Champaign: University of Illinois Press, 1999), 94.

"You had the learning in your head": Joyner, *Shared Traditions*, 78

"house boy": U.S. Census Records.

"They pushed their kids hard into education": Shailagh Murray, "A Family Tree Rooted in American Soil," *Washington Post*, October 2, 2008.

"He was a very proud man": Murray, "A Family Tree Rooted in American Soil."

"A lot of times these stories get buried: Murray, "A Family Tree Rooted in American Soil."

"I am married to a black American": Barack Obama, "A More Perfect Union," speech delivered in Philadelphia, Pennsylvania, March 18, 2008.

"An important message": Murray, "A Family Tree Rooted in American Soil."

"There are probably thousands," "It makes more sense to me": Murray, "A Family Tree Rooted in American Soil."

CHAPTER 3

"When [Michelle] applied and came here": Mundy, *Michelle*, 50.

"What would happen if": Cole, "From a Mother's Eyes."

"She badgered and badgered": Yeager, "The Heart and Mind of Michelle Obama."

"focused": Mundy, *Michelle*, 55.

"She didn't goof off": Mundy, *Michelle*, 55.

"I was sort of a goof-off": Mendell, *Obama*, 32.

"just a bunch of kids": Mundy, *Michelle*, 54.

"It was racially diverse": Mundy, *Michelle*, 54.

"a melting pot": Mundy, *Michelle*, 55.

"Willis Wagons": James R. Ralph, *Northern Protest: Martin Luther King, Jr., Chicago, and the Civil Rights Movement* (Cambridge: Harvard University Press, 1993), 20.

"Does everybody here want to go to college?": Yeager, "The Heart and Mind of Michelle Obama."

"What's your first choice?": Mundy, Michelle, 58–59; and others.

"If you pick a college": Bill Reynolds, "He's Much More Than Obama's Brother-in-law," *Providence Journal*, February 10, 2008.

"I knew him, and I knew his study habits": Wolffe, "Barack's Rock."

CHAPTER 4

"Take Catherine out of school": Sally Jacobs, "Learning to Be Michelle Obama," *Boston Globe*, June 15, 2008.

"Catherine is from the South": Brian Feagans, "Georgian Recalls Rooming with Michelle Obama," *Atlanta Journal-Constitution*, April 13, 2008.

"her secret shame": Michael Powell and Jodi Kantor, "After Attacks, Michelle Obama Looks for a New Introduction," *New York Times*, June 18, 2008.

"Sometimes that's the thing you sense": Jacobs, "Learning to Be Michelle Obama."

"I cannot tell you": Jacobs, "Learning to Be Michelle Obama."

"The whole temper and tradition": Mundy, *Michelle*, 61.

Also: Tad Bennicoff, "African Americans and Princeton University: A Brief History," March 11, 2005, Seeley G. Mudd Manuscript Library, Princeton University (www.princeton.edu/mudd/news/faq/topics/African_Americans.shtml).

"He told her it was not possible": Esther Breger, "All Eyes Turn to Michelle Obama '85," *Daily Princetonian*, November 5, 2008.

"overwhelmed": Reynolds, "He's Much More Than Obama's Brother-in-law."

"Mom, Michelle's here telling people": Collins, "The Other Obama."

"did not feel comfortable in the eating clubs": Breger, "All Eyes Turn to Michelle Obama '85."

"[We] did everything the Orthodox students did": Breger, "All Eyes Turn to Michelle Obama '85."

"I could not go a week without hearing that": Jacobs, "Learning to Be Michelle Obama."

"The Third World Center was our life": Jacobs, "Learning to Be Michelle Obama."

"My experiences at Princeton: Michelle Obama, "Princeton-Educated Blacks and the Black Community," thesis submitted for fulfillment of undergraduate degree, Princeton University, Princeton, New Jersey, 1985.

"It was awkward": Mundy, *Michelle*, 76.

"I get that all time from the Chinese kids": Mundy, *Michelle*, 76.

"We weren't sure whether": Wolffe, "Barack's Rock."

"She was not an assimilationist": Breger, "All Eyes Turn to Michelle Obama '85."

CHAPTER 5

"We knew you would do this": Mundy, *Michelle*, 85.

"If I could do this over": Mundy, *Michelle*, 78.

"The thing about these wonderful schools": Johnson, "Michelle Obama's the Natural."

"I had dated a lot of brothers": Mendell, *Obama*, 93–94.

CHAPTER 6

"There would be no reason for me to dislike": Bakst, "Brown Coach Robinson a Strong Voice for Brother-in-law Obama."

"My parents weren't very optimistic": Yeager, "The Heart and Mind of Michelle Obama."

"Lovely": Obama, *Audacity of Hope*, 316.

"I thought, 'Now how would that look?'": Mendell, *Obama*, 94.

"I'm not worrying about dating": West, "Her Plan Went Awry, but Michelle Obama Doesn't Mind."

"She had all these little facts about him": Mundy, *Michelle*, 95.

"Come on": Obama, *Audacity of Hope*, 316.

"Guess what?": Rossi, "Obama's Anchor."

"First impression": Mark Patinkin, "Obama's Got Game, Says Brother-in-law," *Providence Journal*, March 1, 2008.

"We gave it a month": Johnson, "Michelle Obama's the Natural."

"He was just another one": Henneberger, "Michelle Obama Interview: Her Father's Daughter."

"My father and I had a theory," "Oh, no": Johnson, "Michelle Obama's the Natural."

"I was happy to report," "he was confident": Patinkin,
   "Obama's Got Game, Says Brother-in-law."
"My sister is one tough girl": Bill Reynolds, "Welcome to
   Obama's Family," *Providence Journal*, February 15, 2007.
"He was able to articulate a vision": Gwen Ifill, "Michelle
   Obama: Beside Barack," *Essence*, August 2008.
"He could've gone to Wall Street": Jay Newton-Small,
   "Michelle's Savvy Sacrifice," *Time*, August 25, 2008.
"He talked about the simple notion": Henneberger,
   "Michelle Obama Interview: Her Father's Daughter."
"There was a glimmer": Obama, *Audacity of Hope*, 317.
"We would have this running debate": Collins, "The Other
   Obama."

CHAPTER 7
"If I died in four months," "You can make money": Wolffe,
   "Barack's Rock."
"she would have been a superstar": Rossi, "Obama's Anchor."
"I looked out at my neighborhood": Powell and Kantor,
   "After Attacks, Michelle Obama Looks for a New
   Introduction."
"Don't you want to pay": Newton-Small, "Michelle's Savvy
   Sacrifice."
"I'm sure at Sidley": Newton-Small, "Michelle's Savvy
   Sacrifice."
"I did exactly": Mary Mitchell, "'A Girl from the South Side'
   Talks," *Chicago Sun-Times*, August 5, 2007.
"I offered her a job": Wolffe, "Barack's Rock."
"At a time when": Newton-Small, "Michelle's Savvy
   Sacrifice."
"It sounded risky": Wolffe, "Barack's Rock."

"She had incredibly high expectations": Yeager, "The Heart and Mind of Michelle Obama."

"We had a big gala": Collins, "The Other Obama."

"She let nothing slide": Powell and Kantor, "After Attacks, Michelle Obama Looks for a New Introduction."

"Real change": Powell and Kantor, "After Attacks, Michelle Obama Looks for a New Introduction."

"She built it to last": Rossi, "Obama's Anchor."

CHAPTER 8

"I grew up five minutes": Yeager, "The Heart and Mind of Michelle Obama."

"My wife's anger": Obama, *Audacity of Hope*, 328.

"I spent a lot of time": Johnson, "Michelle Obama's the Natural."

"I'm loving every day": Reynolds, "He's Much More Than Obama's Brother-in-law."

"The big issue around the Senate": Mendell, *Obama*, 151–52.

"Just don't screw it up, buddy": Obama, *Audacity of Hope*, 359.

"There's not a liberal America": Barack Obama, Remarks to Democratic National Convention, Boston, Massachusetts, July 27, 2004.

"Daddy, are you going to be," "Well, Senator": Mendell, *Obama*, 303–4.

CHAPTER 9

"I'd like to teach": Mendell, *Obama*, 101.

"I took myself down": Ifill, "Michelle Obama: Beside Barack."

"Eventually I thought": Henneberger, "Michelle Obama Interview: Her Father's Daughter."

"Yeah, I'm a little tired": Ifill, "Michelle Obama: Beside Barack."

"Michelle is such a disciplinarian": Johnson, "Michelle Obama's the Natural."

"It's harder for him": Yeager, "The Heart and Mind of Michelle Obama."

"Occasionally, it gives people heartburn": Collins, "The Other Obama."

"You are amazed": Powell and Kantor, "After Attacks, Michelle Obama Looks for a New Introduction."

"I'd have to think about that": *Good Morning America*, ABC News, February 4, 2008.

"It's like I can't think out loud": Wolffe, "Barack's Rock."

"for the first time": Michelle Obama, Remarks at campaign stop in Milwaukee, Wisconsin, February 18, 2008.

"When a team is down": Patinkin, "Obama's Got Game, Says Brother-in-law."

"magical . . . Tinkerbell": Kristen Gelineau, "Would-be First Lady Drifts into Rock Star Territory," Associated Press, March 30, 2008.

"I don't think I can": Richard Wolffe, "I Can Only Be Who I Can Be," *Newsweek*, February 25, 2008.

"Barack and I": Michelle Obama, Remarks at the Democratic National Convention, August 25, 2008.